THE NEW EXECUTIVE ASSISTANT

ADVICE FOR SUCCEEDING IN YOUR CAREER

MELBA J. DUNCAN

McGraw-Hill
New York San Francisco Washington, D.C. Auckland Bogotá
Caracas Lisbon London Madrid Mexico City Milan
Montreal New Delhi San Juan Singapore
Sydney Tokyo Toronto

Library of Congress Cataloging-in-Publication Data

Duncan, Melba J.
The new executive assistant : advice for succeeding in your career / Melba J. Duncan.
p. cm.
Includes index.
ISBN 0-07-018241-8 (pbk.)
1. Middle managers. 2. Executive ability. 3. Success in business. I. Title.
HD38.2.D86 1996
658.4'3—dc21 96-51841
CIP

McGraw-Hill

A Division of The ***McGraw-Hill*** *Companies*

9 10 QPF/QPF 0 5 4

ISBN 0-07-018241-8

The sponsoring editor for this book was Betsy Brown, the editing supervisor was Penny Linskey, and the production supervisor was Claire B. Stanley. It was set in Fairfield by Victoria Khavkina of McGraw-Hill's Professional Book Group composition unit.

Printed and bound by Quebecor/Book Press.

This book is printed on recycled, acid-free paper containing a minimum of 50% recycled, de-inked fiber.

Dedication:
To Your Career

CONTENTS

PREFACE: WHY YOU NEED THIS BOOK

The role of the professional executive assistant is in transition. This book will help you make sense of the main features of this inherently unpredictable and highly rewarding position.

Questions abound: What title accurately identifies the role? What is the nature of the position? What opportunities for personal development exist within this position? What are appropriate salaries for the level of responsibilities we are expected to assume?

The answers to these questions—and dozens of others—are all frustratingly vague, and to the extent that we are able to answer them, we can do so only imperfectly, and on an ongoing basis with frequent revisions. The ambiguous nature of the work is both frustrating (because it leads some outsiders to undervalue our contributions) and exciting (because those who learn to relish this line of work do so out of a love for the challenges associated with constant change). We derive satisfaction from the mutually rewarding relationships we create—and at the same time we enjoy the virtually unlimited opportunities for intellectual and emotional growth offered by this position (the horizontal fast track, with its tough standards to be met at the same level).

In this Preface, I want to take a brief look at the issues and historical patterns that I believe will be offset by the continuing evolution of this role.

TECHNOLOGY—PROS AND CONS

The current generation of senior executives fully expect assistants to be well versed in the ever-changing world of office technologies. This perspective is based on several underlying assumptions, all of which are, to some extent, erroneous.

Without a working understanding of computers (an understanding some executives still lack), senior managers tend to believe the hype they receive from technology managers about the ease and use and functionality of systems. Consequently, they have unrealistic expectations. They often believe that bringing about dramatic changes in the way an assistant stores, organizes, and retrieves information is fundamentally no more complex than, say, changing typewriters. Anyone familiar with the learning curve associated with new technology will readily recognize the fallacy here.

Mastery of these devices is a process, not an event. Substantial training is required, followed by the opportunity to practice the new skills in a supportive environment. Learning and understanding then occur, and one is able to incorporate the new tools into the current paradigm.

The fantasy is that the new system more or less instantly increases everyone's productivity once it's installed. The reality is more familiar. Let's look at what really happens. An assistant walks into work one day and a new computer system sits on the desk, accompanied by a manual written in computerspeak. There may be a note attached to the system from someone in another department, informing the assistant how lucky she is to have this technology, and boasting about how easy it's going to make everyone's workday. Maybe the assistant received some training on this system—three months ago, for a couple of hours. Maybe she didn't.

After coming in early and working late for a few weeks to learn the system, the assistant may finally gain enough confidence to use the software for productive work. That's when the gremlins of computing get to work. Has anyone ever seen a computer system crash during a training system, with an instructor nearby to sort things out? I never have. Crashes, of course, only occur when there is some significant event looming—a board meeting, say—that requires the use of information within the system. All the preparatory work for the Big Meeting is locked away inside a mass of plastic and glass that is blinking an error message with a level of consistency and unyielding effort that would impress a Zen Buddhist.

So, the assistant calls the 48-hour-a-day emergency hotline, only to receive a voice-mail message, delivered in soothing tones, informing her that the entire service department is at a training session learning how to "keep the customer #1 on the priority list."

That's the real world (or at least a fair approximation of it). It's easy to see how assistants are less than elated when people start talking about the many and varied benefits of "cutting-edge technology." The other major concern is that, even when the systems do work as designed, they are often cumbersome, illogical and lead to situations where they actually take more time to use than the manual systems they were designed to replace. Systems analysts, alas, often overlook one small aspect of systems design, namely the step that involves validating the usability of the final product with the people who will actually use the systems. Is it any surprise that some people actually keep computers on their desks for display—but continue to use the manual systems that have served them so well for many years?

A side note: I would encourage senior executives to walk the halls and listen to the comments users make about the actual productivity increases that have (or haven't) been achieved through the use of technology. What users say often differs substantially from the summaries provided by information technology managers.

On balance, this does not mean that the tens of millions of dollars spent on office computing have been spent in vain. The message, rather, is this: It is high time to apply common sense to the design and implementation of the products, and to the training and support of users. It is also time to introduce a little more realism to the expectations of senior management about real-world productivity increases, and the amount of time it will take to achieve them.

PERSON TO PERSON

The ability to keep a team or a project in focus, to bring an initiative to fruition through strategic time and personnel management, are now vital elements for the career of the successful executive assistant.

Today's executive assistant requires a high degree of strategic skill. Effectiveness on the job is increasingly tied to *correct choices*. And what we choose to do, it turns out, is as important as the choices we make about what *not* to do. Constant discipline and clear communication of day-to-day decisions are necessary in order to sustain career momentum and an advantage on the job. Self-motivated creativity, highly developed perceptual skills, the ability to spot problems before they occur, and an understanding of information systems—all of these are prerequisites for career success, now and in the future.

A WORD OR TWO ON AGE AND WEIGHT DISCRIMINATION

Contrary to what we would hope to be the case, today's executive assistant is very likely to encounter blatant age and weight discrimination.

There remains the misguided, all-too-popular belief that younger assistants are preferable to older ones because they are quicker learners, able to adapt more easily to computers, more flexible on the job, and unlikely to be "bossy." How do we address these preconceptions—beyond simply acknowledging their existence?

The best answer may be to constantly remind ourselves about what the stereotypes are and use our on-the-job—or interview—performance to overcome them. How? By demonstrating open-mindedness, flexibility, and tact. We should also be aware that we are responsible for maintaining an impeccable personal appearance. We may not be able to look twenty years younger (or, for that matter, drop thirty pounds) overnight, but we do have the power to choose how we look and how we present ourselves.

Hiring executives, too—and those who represent them—also have some responsibilities. They owe it to themselves and their organization to find and retain the very best person for the position, even if that person is somewhat older than other candidates or slightly heavier than the average applicant.

ONGOING EFFORT

A commitment to continuous self-improvement is a must for the executive assistant. Flexibility and relentless effort are the best forms of practice. The intellectual skills developed on the job are the result of the ongoing search for new ways to adapt to change.

The successful executive assistant must commit to learning to do many new things well, and in short order. Adapting gracefully to change is among the most important tasks to master.

THE PROFILE

How can a position with such varied and challenging responsibilities be so undervalued? It takes exceptional people to do this job well. The executive assistant's job is much more arduous than most people suppose.

Those who do not truly understand the nature of this position attach competence and "fit" labels based on narrow grounds, such as the type of businesses reflected in a work history, or the number of words typed per minute, or some other such "secretarial" skill. Little consideration is given to the subtle demands of the position being filled, the capacity of a candidate to learn (much, if not most, of the learning is on the job), or the personal values of the applicant. Even less attention is given to social assurance, good manners, and the display of temperament, attitude, and inclination appropriate to the position.

In the matching process, the key to success in this position is in the proper alignment of the executive assistant to the personality and needs of the hiring executive and the organization. But there is much more to consider. Is the individual grounded in sound principles that encourage self-development? Does she have a broad understanding of human nature? Is she tolerant? Is she capable of overcoming unexpected challenges in a proactive way?

The valued executive assistant welcomes the opportunity to be of service to others. The *wrong* person for this position is one who misuses power, acts out of a false sense of entitlement, or is willing to sabotage colleagues and management out of self-interest.

When trying to place people in the executive assistant position, recruiters often lose sight of the ability to value differences, the willingness to develop and maintain healthy relationships, and the type of self-discipline and desire to succeed usually associated with successful executive assistants. All of these qualities, I would argue, are essential to success in this job.

Integrity, too, is often undervalued by recruiters. The executive assistant is routinely entrusted with highly confidential information about the organization *and* the person to whom she reports. Obviously, a firm sense of discretion, judgment, and an unshakable set of personal ethics, are essential when handling sensitive information on a daily basis.

Climbing in this career means being clear about your personal goals, learning how to add value, and developing skills you can take anywhere.

THIS BOOK WILL HELP YOU...

- learn more about the specifics of this challenging position, and determine whether it really is right for you.
- develop or strengthen the "mindset" necessary for success

within this field: an outlook that rejects notions of entitlement or short-term advantage, and focuses instead on service and support.

- learn how to add value to each interaction you experience during the day.
- establish realistic goals that will help you pursue a rewarding career path.

Achievement and opportunity within this position fall to those whose *total* performance has earned them the respect and confidence of others in high places. If this book helps you move closer to making contributions that earn that level of respect, it will have succeeded in its aim.

Melba Duncan

ACKNOWLEDGMENTS

Many people helped me to develop and refine this book. I would like to express my thanks to my agent, Bert Holtje, to Brandon Toropov, David Nisbet, the staff and clients of The Duncan Group, and all the good people at McGraw-Hill, who worked very hard to get this book into your hands: my patient and supportive editor Betsy Brown, Penny Linskey of Professional Publishing and Patricia Fagan and Alberta Esposito, who personify the Executive Assistant of the future.

Special acknowledgment should be made of the influence of the hundreds of senior managers and executive assistants I have had the privilege of working with over the years. Without their input and support, this book would not have come into existence.

My very special thanks and appreciation to my husband, Max Rodriguez, and my daughter, Michelle Devlin, for their patience, encouragement and inspiration.

INTRODUCTION

To have begun is to have done half the task.

—Horace

There's a lot more to the executive assistant's job than typing and shorthand.

Many of the executives we run into at the Duncan Group—people who are looking for executive assistants—have an incomplete idea of what this career is all about. They understand what needs to be completed by the end of the day, but they don't understand the personal chemistry necessary to bring about those events.

It turns out that a good personality "fit" with the executive in question is the single most important factor in determining the success of the relationship. More important than background. More important than work history. More important than word processing speed. That's important for people in hiring positions to know, of course, but it's also important for you to bear in mind as you consider the future path of your career.

In addition, we've found that both parties—the assistant and the executive—need to have a solid knowledge of themselves at some level in order for the partnership to work. Why? Because self-knowledge usually means better communication, and communication supports that "good fit" on any number of levels. If either partner understands the executive assistant's job only at a conceptual level, as something that is task-oriented or that doesn't require interaction with another person on a one-on-one level, there's a good chance that both partners' needs will go unmet. As you're about to find out, this is an extraordinary career, one in which the challenges are constant and the logistical hurdles immense. The best way to succeed in this career—or, for that matter, to hire someone who will succeed in it—is to take full advantage of an environment in which unique contributions are the result of a self-aware, partnership-oriented work pattern.

More simply, the successful executive assistant is not a subordinate, but a business ally of the first order, one with a strong sense of purpose and mission. When both partners understand this, the results can be spectacular.

It's my hope that this book will help point you toward the next stage of your career growth. But a book can serve only as a tool—and because each reader's situation is different, an imperfect one at that. In taking advantage of the advice that appears on the following pages, you will need to make use of an even more important tool, one that can be customized to your own needs and habits, one that will pave the way toward peak achievement. That tool is *you*, and more specifically, the thoughts you use to create your world.

> As people start to recognize that their thoughts create their experience of life moment to moment, they simultaneously start to experience freedom. Freedom to create, to feel content, to drop old habits. Freedom to experience life and relationships anew. Thought and thought alone determines our experience of life. Through this understanding we can increasingly enjoy the vagaries of life.
>
> —Judith A. Sedgeman, M.S.

It's important to find the right job, the right manager, the right atmosphere, the right work environment, the right company. But it's also important to find the right *you*, because with the right *you*, any world is possible.

May the world you create be the perfect one.

Melba Duncan

TIPS FOR SUCCESS

A desperate outlook is a choice we make. Peace is simply another one.

Be compulsive about details.

It can be done!

Don't repeat the same error.

The only measure for success is performance.

Develop a positive vision. Believe that the universe is governed by an Absolute Goodness. Be grateful.

Encourage others to do their best; make others feel important.

Be a troubleshooter, problem solver, as well as a doer.

Treat yourself as if you are the most important asset you'll ever have. Aren't you?

Admit mistakes.

Don't let your ego get in the way of a sincere "I'm sorry."

When you fail, don't give up.

CHAPTER ONE

THE CHANGING WORLD OF TODAY'S EXECUTIVE ASSISTANT

If we are to attain the empowerment we crave, we must accept responsibility for both our own roles and the roles of our leaders. Only by accepting this dual responsibility do we ultimately accept responsibility for our organizations and the people they serve.

—IRA CHALEFF, *THE COURAGEOUS FOLLOWER*

Is this book for you?

It is if you either want to become an executive assistant or are one already and hope to make the most of your career potential.

In the early part of this book, we'll take a brief look at the challenges and rewards offered in this existing occupation—and discuss some of the reasons the job is fundamentally different today from what it was just a few years ago. Today's executive assistant is, it turns out, as much a partner as a subordinate, as much a source of inspiration as a manager of schedules and phone calls, as much an independent communicator as a relayer of the thoughts and views of a top manager.

In later chapters we'll talk about your job search, discuss the importance adaptability plays in the face of constant change, and look at the best ways to ensure your success within this position over the long term.

A FEW WORDS ABOUT TITLES AND DUTIES

Let me share something with you at the outset: I'm not crazy about the title *executive assistant.* It places a great deal of emphasis on the notion of "assisting," and not enough—for my taste at any rate—on the idea of summoning one's personal creative resources. The necessity for reliance on personal creativity and innovation is more important now than it ever has been for this job. In fact, in today's work environment creativity is perhaps the most important quality you can possess if you hope to succeed in this line of work. The career is just too difficult for someone who can't bring a creative approach to its many challenges!

The title of executive assistant doesn't convey a tenth of the importance of the role, or give any inkling of the combined perspicacity, inventiveness, flexibility, poise, and resourcefulness this person brings to the organization for which she works. (By the way, because the majority of executive assistants are female, I'm going to use the female pronoun, simply because doing so is more convenient and sounds better than writing "she/he"or some other such formulation. I certainly don't want to leave anyone with the impression, however, that men are not welcome in this role, or that they do not perform superlatively within it.)

The position we will be discussing, then—the one in which you serve as the eyes and ears of a senior official, resolve logistical problems related to that official's work, and monitor a variety of important initiatives with others in the organization for him or her—is generally known as that of an executive assistant. I much prefer a new title we've developed in my office: *executive coordinator.* This phrase offers a better sense of the facilitating, order-imparting nature of this challenging, rewarding position. The truth is that the workers in this category—and many of the workers in the positions that lead up to it—do a great deal more coordinating, managing the flow of information and projects, and organizing and facilitating than assisting.

The organizations that thrive in the new economy will need, not more clerical workers, but more professionals at every level. What exactly do I mean by "professional"? Michael Hammer, author of *Reengineering the Corporation,* put it this way: "A professional is someone who cares about the result, not just the activity. The only catch is, that takes a certain kind of person." Hammer is suggesting that a true professional is a little bit more of an entrepreneur and a lot less of a simple carrier-out of tasks. That's a standard that everyone in today's customer-first organization is expected to meet, and it's also an idea that the phrase "administrative assistant" or even "executive assistant" really doesn't capture.

Titles make a difference—sometimes a very big difference. The trend away from "secretary" and toward "assistant to Ms. Smith" or "assistant for such-and-such" has gone a long way toward clarifying the increasingly important position that senior administrative people occupy in today's organizations, but I'm afraid the new terminology may not go far enough.

Whenever I have the opportunity, I suggest to business leaders that they consider incorporating the "executive coordinator" title on a broader basis in their organizations. For now, however, it's worth retaining the old terminology, if only out of pragmatism. You are likely to be dealing with an employer or prospective employer who is accustomed to thinking in terms of assistants and support staff, so let's work within those terminologies for the purposes of this book. Please remember, though, that once you've started on your path toward the job you deserve, you may find yourself in a position to lobby for a job title that is a more accurate reflection of the work you do than the human resources handbooks and printouts can offer. Lobby! Do so tactfully, but do it. The name that describes the work you do can have a dramatic impact on your income levels and the later course of your career.

Let's look in detail now at the career path that is likely to lead you to the position that is the subject of this book.

GRADE I: "IS THIS WHERE I START?"

The worker typically known as the executive assistant represents the highest stage on an ascending ladder of responsibility. The first category of worker, which I call Grade I, must be able to respond directly, with some guidance, to any and all requests from management; to handle routine office duties; and to excel at document preparation, using stenography and dictation skills. These workers represent the first rank of administrative support employees. There's certainly no law saying that you must begin at this level as you initiate your career path, but it is certainly true that a good many superior executive assistants have begun their careers with positions that fall into this category.

GRADE II: "HEY, I'M IN CHARGE OF SOMETHING!"

Not surprisingly, the workers at the next grade face greater challenges and enjoy higher levels of compensation. Grade II workers must be able to perform all the Grade I tasks *and* make some key contributions when it comes to time and project management, workflow prioritizing, manage tasks independently, and certain other managerial functions.

Grade II workers must have strong steno transcription skills in order to perform their jobs at a superior level. In addition, they need some knowledge of basic business finance matters. These workers focus more heavily on information and communication management than their Grade I counterparts, and they also have occasional exposure to confidential company materials.

Can you begin your career in a Grade II position? Yes, but it's more common to spend at least a short time in a job that corresponds to the Grade I level.

GRADE III: "I WONDER IF THEY'VE LOOKED AROUND THIS CORNER...?"

As you continue up the ladder, you'll reach Grade III, which receives higher pay than the Grades I and II counterparts. Those at this level must display a certain ability to predict and prevent important logistical problems.

These employees must be able to perform all the Grades I and II tasks, of course, but they must take on significant levels of responsibility in the administrative and managerial areas as well. They are comfortable anticipating needs and even making important decisions. They may offer their managers support in personal areas such as tax coordination, personal banking, and home versus office scheduling. They are occasionally called upon to represent their managers' viewpoints on key issues to others within the organization. The ability to self-manage is the key to success at this level.

GRADE IV: "INDISPENSABLE!"

Grade IV workers—the ones usually known as executive assistants and the ones who receive the most impressive compensation packages—must add to the mix a number of career strengths normally associated with seasoned managerial talent. They must be able to employ strong operating skills, including quality decision-making and problem-solving abilities. They must show significant leadership potential and must have a demonstrated capacity to work independently, plan, organize, coordinate, supplement other skills, and follow through.

They must balance the ability to meet the senior executive's personal and business requirements with the challenge of overseeing administrative staff development and day-to-day performance. They must possess advanced financial skills.

Grade IV workers may be *called* assistants, and they certainly never overshadow their managers—who may be presidents or chief executive officers (CEOs)—but these "assistants" are a long way from being "clerical workers," and everyone of any importance within the organization knows it. Whether or not the organizational chart acknowledges the fact, Grade IV workers are among the most important players in the entire organization.

Outsiders (such as inexperienced salespeople, job seekers, and callow representatives of the media) sometimes make the mistake of considering these workers to be minor functionaries, something akin to a receptionist who happens to work for the Big Cheese. These people could not be more mistaken. When they speak briskly and impatiently to a Grade IV worker, attempt to order her about, or share inappropriate "jokes" in an attempt to intimidate her, they are almost always dooming their cause. The Grade IV worker is the trusted confidante of the top executive: Not only does she manage the chunks of information (including appeals from outsiders!) that make it to the executive's desk, she also is very likely the indispensable coordinator of the boss's nonworking hours. She may well run the organization—or significant parts of it—in the executive's absence.

Some words of warning are in order. If you hope to win a Grade IV position, you should know that the same unpredictable hours, accountability, dedication, and long-term thinking are required of this job as are required of many a senior executive. The truth of the matter is that the effective executive assistant has much more in common with the entrepreneur or CEO than she does with a member of the typing pool or with any of the support workers associated primarily with the fulfillment of repetitive clerical tasks. Those workers are unlikely to be called upon to resolve a pressing personnel problem, or to be pulled out of bed by an emergency overseas phone call at 2:00 A.M. They may claim, and rightly so, that their job description does not incorporate those kinds of challenges. Both the CEO and the assistant who helps guide the workday (and helps avert daily catastrophe) make a commitment to a different kind of outlook on working life. This outlook acknowledges the existence of challenge, uncertainty, and odd hours—and the importance of following through, regardless.

Two scenes from the delightful film *The American President* strike me as worthy of note in any assessment of the duties that accrue to a top-level executive assistant.

The first is one in which Michael Douglas, as the president, is strolling through the White House, his key assistant by his side. As each official visitor or member of the presidential staff passes by, the assistant whispers the person's first name in the chief executive's ear, as well as some current information concerning that individual. The president, without missing a beat, calls out a personalized greeting.

Executive assistants compensate for the weaknesses of their bosses. These days that includes not only covering for the occasional memory lapse—indeed, even predicting and remedying it before it becomes a problem—but also taking the lead when it comes to compensating for any gaps in a manager's technical and information management skills.

The second scene from *The American President* that sums up perfectly the official duties of the contemporary executive assistant occurs when Michael Douglas and Annette Bening, his new girlfriend, are sharing a private moment—one that is interrupted by a sudden crisis that requires the president's immediate attention. Douglas doesn't complain about the existence of a sudden emergency or whine about how the crisis is taking time away from his relationship with Bening. He doesn't struggle against the moment or pretend that his work persona doesn't come into existence until 8:00 A.M. He simply accepts the new reality, tactfully but seamlessly disengages from the moment he and his loved one are sharing, and puts on his "time to get to work" face.

The fictional president's poise in transition is one that successful people in all arenas of the business world, and executive assistants in particular, must learn to emulate, both in integrating their private lives with the demands of the business day and in prioritizing the various challenges their professional responsibilities bring about.

Executive assistants, in other words, make poised, seamless transitions. These days it means that they manage a demanding work schedule, take pleasure in their nonwork life as circumstances allow, and help keep track of a number of organizational and team-related initiatives at the same time. (In many workplaces, the executive assistant is one of the prime movers in the successful coordination of the various work teams acting to fulfill the vision and goals of the top executive.) Being able to transfer easily between the various formal elements of your job, without getting distracted or flustered, is an essential skill.

"Sounds Like My Kind of Job! How Do I Get It"

We've examined the four main categories that lead to the executive assistant's job. As I've indicated, it's *possible* to enter the progression at the Grade II level, but honesty compels me to

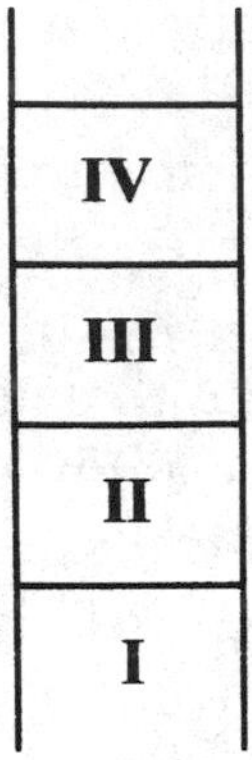

observe once again that, strictly as a statistical matter, it's not *likely.* (Making a commitment to ongoing learning can have an effect here.) Having said that, I call your attention to the "ladder," which describes the typical career path for an executive assistant.

Now, if you're like most of us, you want your career to progress, not stand still. And if you're reading this book, it's a very good bet that you're doing so in the hope of reaching that fourth level. It follows, then, that if you're on the Grade I rung, your objective is to progress to Grade II; if you're at Grade II, your objective is to move up to Grade III; and if you're working at the Grade III level, you hope to move up to Grade IV. Here's a breakdown of the tasks that face you, depending on where you currently stand on the ladder.

If you are seeking to gain entry to a position in the Grade I category, you will need to have experience and/or training in the following areas:

- Organizational skills
- Ability to resolve differences and maintain relationships at all levels
- Solid Social Skills
- Impeccable character (integrity, consistency, discretion)

- Flexible, "do what it takes, deliver what is asked" attitude, regardless of formal dictates of job description
- Good team orientation and interpersonal skills
- Heightened awareness and curiosity
- Ability to maintain a professional relationship based on trust, impeccable judgment, and discretion
- Ability to manage confidential information
- Excellent proofreading ability
- Stenography and dictation skills
- Computer literacy, willingness to learn new systems
- Ability to establish priorities
- Ability to communicate effectively, orally, and on paper

If you are hoping to move from a Grade I to a Grade II category, you will also need to have experience and/or training in these areas:

- Planning and coordinating abilities
- Time/project management
- Supervisory skills, including ability to explain new systems to others
- Basic financial skills
- Organization and prioritization abilities
- Ability to sense requirements, communicate effectively, and follow up
- Ability to manage multiple tasks and perform under pressure
- Ability to follow up on assignments, including handling the most mundane details

If you are hoping to move from a Grade II to a Grade III category, you will also need to have experience and/or training in these areas:

- Hands-on managerial skills
- Ability to help assess new systems

- Ability to weigh importance of various tasks
- Thorough knowledge of organization and its working patterns
- Multiple household/residence management, including hiring staff
- Ability to arrange and coordinate projects with outsiders (bankers, architects, and so on)

Finally, if you are hoping to move from Grade III to the Grade IV executive assistant category, you will also need to have experience and/or training in these areas:

- Superior "change management" skills
- Ability to help plan and execute implementation of new systems
- Advanced financial skills
- Advanced information management skills
- Leadership and team-building skills
- Personnel management
- Human resources skills
- Awareness of diversity
- General knowledge of industry and world events
- Business sense
- Interpersonal competence (openness and approachability)
- Persistence

Success in all four grades requires a certain discipline: a tough-minded pursuit of the facts, a willingness to keep digging for the information necessary to support a good decision. Discipline may also take the form of skepticism for what is conventionally considered "not doable." When someone says that a particular task is impossible, a good executive assistant should ask herself, "Why?"

OVERCOMING SKILL GAPS

Assuming that you don't have a mentor who's willing to see to it that your skills are developed in the way they're meant to be, how do you get past a gap in one or more of the background areas you need to make progress on the ladder? The answer may lie in one of three areas.

The first is probably the most traditional approach: studying through a local educational institution. Is there a community college or other establishment you can work into your routine? You may decide to take night classes in a new word processing or spreadsheet program, or in business administration, or management and place the accompanying certification or class credit on your résumé. If time or finances do not permit this, don't give up entirely on the idea of taking advantage of an appropriate academic outlet. Why not arrange to *audit* a course—at no cost—and upgrade your skills in that way? The scheduling may be easier (in that you won't be penalized if you have to miss a day or two for other commitments, and you may be able to make up the material covered at your own pace), and you certainly can't beat the cost. While it's true that you can't really boast too much on your résumé about classes you've taken as an auditor, you can certainly make mention of these sessions during a face-to-face interview. Showing that you've taken such an initiative is one of the best ways I know of to impress a prospective employer.

The second way to overcome a skill gap is even easier to work into your schedule: Hit the library. Your local public library probably has hundreds of resources available to you on a wide variety of topics, including the most recent software training books. Also, a good reference librarian will be able to point you toward recent articles of interest about the industry you're targeting and toward textbooks on business administration, marketing, accounting, and virtually any other area you feel you need to develop.

The third method for learning something you need? Well, it's not for the faint of heart, but it certainly has a long and proud history. *Volunteer to take on a tough project and pick up what you need to know on the fly.* Let's say you currently work in a Grade II job, and you're interested in expanding your skill base enough to make a move to a Grade III job possible in the near future. Rather than waiting for a company training program to come along (it may never do so), raise your hand and volunteer to tackle a project no one else at your level is eager to deal with, one that will expose you to some of the tasks you'll need to master in order to make the move to the next level. We learn by doing, right? So get out there and do! As long as there's someone in your workplace to whom you can appeal for advice and (occasional) support when things get tricky, you may be in a perfect position to expand your skill base and pick up brownie points at the same time.

Let me take a moment to address an underlying principle that may make that third option seem a little less intimidating. We live in an information age; almost all the work we do, no matter what the field, intersects in some way with a computer or other information management system. The nice thing about working with today's systems is that they are almost exclusively *pictorial* in approach—they're built around pictures of things you click on with your mouse. That means they're designed to make browsing and experimenting and finding your way around the program relatively painless. Maybe not always perfect. But relatively painless. That's not to say that you can develop instant competence with a particular program by clicking a mouse two or three times, but you certainly *can* find your way around the main features of a good contemporary software program without too much difficulty. For instance, if you need to get up to speed on a new spreadsheet program, there's a very good chance that you can do so more or less on your own.

If you have a strong hesitation when it comes to learning new applications "on the fly," you may not be cut out to be an executive assistant in the technologically based economy in which we live.

Here's another way of saying the same thing: *Learning how to make* some *sense of unfamiliar computers and/or software—or any number of other technological resources—is an essential skill of the new executive assistant.* Thanks to the graphical design interface of the Macintosh and Windows operating systems, as well as any number of computer technologies, this is not at all difficult to do, as long as you keep your initial goals modest and your outlook optimistic. People who constantly tell themselves "I can't figure out computer systems unless someone trains me first" are creating a self-fulfilling, and self-limiting prophecy. Don't be one of them.

KEYS TO PERFORMANCE: WHAT IT TAKES TO MAKE AN IMPACT AS AN EXECUTIVE ASSISTANT (OR FOR THAT MATTER, AN ASPIRING ONE)

The formal qualifications of the job are not, of course, the only issues you must address if you wish to succeed as an executive assistant. If you hope to enter this field, you have chosen one of the most complex, demanding, unpredictable lines of work imaginable, due in no small measure to a single, sobering fact: It is often the executive assistant who must take a lead role when it comes to adapting to the ramifications of technological change. (We'll deal with this topic in depth a little later on.)

Add to that fact the bewildering variety of work demands, which I must warn you are more or less impossible to codify or formalize. Despite the existence of written job descriptions, this position generally boils down to an injunction to "keep things from going wrong." The position you want, in other words, is one whose most notable element is its lack of formal boundaries, and one that places an unusual emphasis on change.

Yet I firmly believe that when you get right down to it, change—especially change that has uncertainty based on technological advances at its heart—is a positive experience for the executive assistant. Change often incorporates transition and progress, even if it may not always feel like that. At times, I admit, change feels more like a rocky ride over a waterfall! But trust me, you'll go further embracing change in your work as an executive assistant than you will in rejecting it.

Beyond the technical skills appearing on the list, what are the hallmarks of effectiveness for this irreplaceable worker? What are the characteristics that make it likely that you'll rise on that ladder, or succeed at the highest possible level once you reach the top rung?

In addition to serving as the buffer for much of the technological change her organization must accommodate, the successful executive assistant must be the kind of team player and role model that author Ira Chaleff refers to as the "courageous follower": someone who is utterly accountable, who has a clear personal concept of mission, who is capable of questioning initiatives tactfully when they seem headed for problems, and who nevertheless works in an orbit in which a top official occupies the undisputed central position. Such a person must display tact, humor, perseverance, diplomacy, and, as I have mentioned before and will mention again, no small degree of creativity to be truly effective, and to make a real impact on the job.

And IMPACT is what it all comes down to. In my view there are six keys to maximum productivity for the successful—and sought-after—executive assistant, keys that are embodied in the initial letters of the word IMPACT.

THE FIRST KEY: THE "I" IN IMPACT STANDS FOR INFORMATION EXPERTISE

This "information" aspect of success on the job has to do with deftly managing the newest information technology, but also with the often challenging task of serving as the eyes and ears of one's manager. That means channeling out what is inessential, channeling in what must be reviewed, keeping up with industry trends as well as domestic and foreign affairs (because we are operating within a global economy), and developing an ability to keep up relations with key people in the organization.

Because of the immense worldwide significance of recent technological advances, we'll be discussing in some detail the phenomenal power that today's information management equipment places at your disposal. We'll also take a look at some of the ways the very dynamic of working has changed as a result of technological advances, and examine some strategies for making sense of the high-tech aspect of today's professional world.

Bear in mind that getting the right information in the first place means maintaining a network that includes virtually all the people with whom your manager comes in contact. Contrary to the old adage, in the information age both what you know and whom you know count for a great deal. In fact, what you know often *governs* whom you know, and vice versa!

THE SECOND KEY: THE "M" IN IMPACT STANDS FOR MATURITY

If there were ever a job in which it was advisable to check your ego at the door, it is this one. Tact, balance, discipline, judgment, and discretion are essential elements of the executive assistant's job.

This is not a job for the thin-skinned. People who make a habit of taking things personally may succeed in any number of endeavors, but I think I can say without too much fear of contradiction that they're not likely to be happy or effective as executive assistants.

You can't afford the luxury of tit-for-tat. Tit-for-tat uses up too much energy! When your manager blows his top after a long day, or says something to you that shows temporary evidence of more aggravation than wit, or forgets a set of instructions he's passed along and contradicts himself, you *must* (repeat, *must*) avoid the temptation to file these incidents for use in a later "get back at the boss" session, either with your manager or through someone else. You *must* avoid the temptation to take things personally. If you betray confidences, you will undermine an occasionally stressful, but normal, working environment, destroy the level of trust on which the relationship is based—and run the risk of short-circuiting your own career.

Maturity on the job means gossiping is out, period. It also means proper etiquette, due courtesy, and a healthy dose of common sense when carrying out requests that affect others in the organization. The effective executive assistant knows that when the CEO asks her to "get that incompetent batch of know-nothings in marketing up here for a meeting," a fair translation is in order.

THE THIRD KEY: THE "P" IN IMPACT STANDS FOR POLITICAL SKILLS

As I've mentioned, the executive assistant is very often one of the most important players in the whole organization. Just as a senior executive would be well advised to develop alliance-building and coalition-management skills, so the executive assistant should spend time developing these interpersonal abilities.

In my opinion, a charismatic, personable executive assistant with unquenchable integrity is far more likely to deliver results for her manager and her organization than any number of Dragon Ladies. If you think that one of the perks of occupying a position of influence within the organization is the right to make enemies when the mood strikes you, think again. Your manager won't stand for that—and you shouldn't, either, because enemy formation is one of the best ways to stunt your own career growth.

Even a loud and quarrelsome team member is still a team member whose suggestions, in all likelihood, carry both pros and cons that are worthy of examination. The effective executive assistant learns how to channel the instincts and observations of the difficult people with whom she and her manager work, helping make sure that no good idea goes overlooked simply because of some personality-related problem. At the same time she smooths the way so that her manager spends as little time as possible—ideally, none at all—in nonproductive exchanges with people who simply like to hear themselves talk.

For the executive assistant, good political skills very often take the form of readiness to step back when credit is assigned to others. Because the executive assistant is acting on behalf of a manager, learning when and how to broadcast personal successes is a matter of ongoing experience. With the right executive you'll find a victory that you both win is a shared triumph *and* an investment in your personal career development.

The Fourth Key: The "A" in IMPACT Stands for Adaptability

Change, as we have seen earlier and will note again, is a constant for today's executive assistant. In fact, change may well be the *only* constant in the contemporary business world. The effective executive assistant must adapt to changes in technology, in organizational structures, in management styles, and not infrequently, in today's ever-shifting markets. Among the many dangers of focusing on the narrow limits of a formal job description is the overriding one that job descriptions may become obsolete with staggering speed these days!

Fortunately, adaptability carries extraordinary career benefits. The development of experience relevant to a wide variety of situations, and an eventual emphasis on the transferability of skills in the matching process, means that career opportunity across industries is virtually unlimited for the executive assistant.

The capable executive assistant knows that she is of greatest value to her organization when she adopts the mindset of the *generalist,* the person who establishes a solid level of competence in a number of different disciplines, technical or otherwise. From a distance, there may seem to be a certain safety in being the only person in the company who knows every single answer to every possible question that may come up for a particular system. But remember that systems don't stick around forever! Remember, too, that some of the tasks you'll be asked to perform temporarily—specifically, leadership and decision-making tasks that put an emphasis on dealing with the unpredictable—may be the very ones by which you are judged. A recent article in *Executive Edge* cited a Gibbs Report survey of Fortune 500 companies which found that *one-half* of key administrative personnel are evaluated on their leadership abilities. The same article reported that "76 percent of senior managers say their secretary plays a 'very' or 'somewhat important' role in the decision-making process on a daily basis."

As we'll see in a later chapter of this book, your best shot at becoming indispensable lies in mastering the art of *adapting* to new opportunities, systems, organizational structures, and procedures, rather than in attempting to develop an encyclopedic knowledge of a particular piece of software, organizational flowchart, or product/service line. Set as your goal a pragmatic level of competence in a *whole lot* of different areas. In the end, the only task for which you may need to develop top-to-bottom, A-to-Z mastery is the ability to act in an inspired way when presented with a new set of facts.

Committing to adaptability means committing to being one of the people who has an *impact* on the organization's direction, one of the people with influence.

Committing to adaptability means developing a wide range of masteries—not just one or two.

THE FIFTH KEY: THE "C" IN IMPACT STANDS FOR COMMUNICATION

Establishing a nonthreatening working vocabulary between yourself and the key people in the organization is of critical importance. Executive assistants often work in extremely high-pressure situations; the ability to get a point across quickly, concisely, and without ruffling feathers is essential, as is the ability to uncover critical information that may assist in your manager's endeavor.

This item, closely related to the "Information" skill described above, is nevertheless distinct from it because it emphasizes an ability too many people lose sight of: "honing" one's message. The idea is to shape and target important facts so that they reach, and interest, the recipient. You may recall from the classic comic strip "Peanuts," Lucy Van Pelt's noble attempt to provide all her acquaintances with a detailed listing of their various faults. For some strange reason people didn't react well to this technique!

Outlining what people are doing wrong does not constitute good communication, even if all the points you cite are correct! The effective executive assistant will recognize that different messages can mean different things to different people, and she will master the difficult art of "selling" the same set of facts to disparate audiences in very different ways. She also knows that assuming the informal position as spokesperson for a top official carries certain special demands and that there will be times when she will need to reject the temptation to speak as freely as other members of the organization are wont to do. Learning to translate statements and initiatives into terms that won't double back on one's manager (or oneself) and learning to address other team members in a way that encourages them to respond constructively are key challenges and imperative skills.

Developing good communication skills is a long-term effort and one that demands continuous attention.

THE SIXTH KEY: THE "T" IN IMPACT STANDS FOR TAKING INITIATIVE

Initiative is perhaps the most difficult and elusive of the six keys for effectiveness. The ability to discern when it's essential to assume a more direct role in this job is not the accomplishment of a single day or a few simple rules; instead, it is a lifelong balancing act, one that depends on the people with whom we are working, the circumstances we are facing directly, and, just as important, the emotional atmosphere in the room. Keen judgment and discretion are a must when it comes to knowing when to act decisively—and when not to.

One thing is certain: An informed executive assistant has a responsibility to speak up tactfully if a looming crisis is likely to go unnoticed. The ability to anticipate problems on the horizon, and take action by alerting others about that trouble, is one of the most important assets an informed executive assistant brings to the table. Not surprisingly, it is also one of the reasons people who do well in this job tend to have an excellent profile for top management positions.

How do you know when to step forward? Beyond staying informed, knowing who the key players are, and showing understanding when it comes to sensitive relationships, there is no simple answer. There are, however, some basic guidelines to follow.

1. If your manager is preoccupied or unavailable because of another matter, but has spoken or written to you in the past about the importance of quick action in a certain area, you

should consider taking the best action you can now and filling in your manager at the earliest opportunity.

2. If you see the potential for imminent and serious legal, public relations, or financial problems for your organization, and you are the only one who can forestall such problems, you should consider taking the best action you can now and filling in your manager (or other appropriate authorities) at the earliest opportunity.
3. If taking decisive action on your manager's behalf is the only way you can expect to resolve a serious, relationship-threatening problem with one of your organization's most important customers, clients, or overseers, then you should consider taking the best action you can now and filling in your manager at the earliest opportunity.

Nothing is written in stone when it comes to crisis management; actions that seem unpopular at the time may later turn out to be very popular indeed, and a slavish attention to the rulebook may, in a fateful situation, result in a black mark against you that proves difficult to erase. Such challenges typically reflect vitally important questions that fall into gray areas, questions that require confidence to resolve, the kind of confidence that is based in a commitment to stay informed. As you attempt to resolve issues as responsibly and conscientiously as possible, bear this in mind: The executive assistant cannot, just as a senior executive cannot, throw up her hands and claim that she did her best. In this job, just as in the other top-level positions of the organization, appropriate action, results, and follow-through are what matter.

Those are, I believe, the six keys for effective work as an executive assistant.

TEMPERAMENT: ARE YOU CUT OUT FOR THIS JOB?

So far we've taken a look at the formal requirements of the job and the six broad operational and interpersonal keys necessary for success within it. There is a third aspect of the work performed by the effective executive assistant that demands close review, and I want to spend a fair amount of time discussing it. That aspect is temperament.

Let me put this next piece of news bluntly, so that there can be no mistake about my sentiments on the matter: This job, although it can be supremely rewarding, is not for everyone.

Some people won't react well to the stresses and challenges inherent in the executive assistant's workday. Some people will bring emotional baggage to the job—trouble dealing with authority figures, for instance—that will make it difficult, if not impossible, for them to hit all the marks. Some people, in short, will be better off trying to find something else to do for a living. Are you one of them? I don't know. But I believe you should look closely at the psychological demands of the job.

I urge you to take a long look at the issue of temperament before you make a serious commitment of time, effort, energy, and money to this career path. In the end, honest self-assessment will be far preferable to trying to make yourself match up with a (very difficult!) job that simply may not be for you.

Do you remember that military recruiting slogan "The few, the proud, the Marines"? That sentiment comes close to capturing the way I feel when I'm asked whether it's possible for *anyone* to succeed in this job. My response is that some of the recruits will have what it takes to make it through boot camp—and others won't. The truth is the successful executive assistant has a very particular initial outlook, or temperament, that is essential to her job. Yes, that means she has a tolerance for things that some people don't much feel like tolerating.

Bear this in mind:

People who have "the right stuff" for becoming executive assistants *enjoy making chaotic situations orderly for their managers*, at virtually any cost, and they don't consider the task of doing so to be something odious. They enjoy the role of providing service.

Put another way, these people have a strong (and unapologetic) detail orientation that inclines unto selflessness. They like catching mistakes, *for the sake of catching mistakes*. Don't misunderstand; this type of detail orientation is not an exercise in scorekeeping. These people don't play "gotcha" or try to prove that they're smarter than anyone else in the organization because they've spotted an error, and they certainly don't engage in mind games with their managers. They strive to smooth out all that can be smoothed out, and they relish doing so.

Let me repeat: *Not everyone in the world of work falls into this category!* If you don't, that's no character failing. It's simply a fact of which you should be aware as you plot out where you want to go from here.

This single character trait—the predisposition toward spotting mistakes and fixing them without making a fuss or expecting special recognition—is so critical to success within this job that I'm going to go out on a limb and say that it is absolutely essential. That may seem like an extreme statement, but I nevertheless believe it to be true.

WHEN IS AN ERROR A CHALLENGE?

There are any number of ways to look at errors and their eradication:

- As proof of our status as intellectual heavyweights once we spot them. (This is best described as the "engineer's mindset.")
- As judgments upon our personal validity. (Insecure team members who balk at the slightest criticism are a good example here.)
- As problems to which other people, generally subordinates, must be attached for reasons of accountability. (In truth, any number of top executives probably fall into this category.)

The successful, fulfilled executive assistant rejects all these approaches to the idea of error. She isn't in the habit of boasting about her troubleshooting capacity; she simply takes action. She never—well, hardly ever—takes reproofs personally; at any rate, she has, or quickly develops, the ability to deflect personal attacks and cut to the heart of a complaint. She never ducks responsibility, even when she might be able to make a good case for doing so.

We are talking about a person who doesn't get rattled by mistakes, but instead learns from them and acts quietly and instinctively to resolve them—or, better yet, prevent them. She enjoys looking around corners and checking behind doors. She is a fanatic about the importance of attention to detail. She focuses on smoothing out what needs to be smoothed out. Period. She *accepts a detail orientation,* from the first moment of her workday to the last. She asks for the spelling of an unfamiliar name and then gets it right from that point forward. She updates erroneous data quickly and without aggravation. She isn't intimidated by the seeming chaos of a busy workday; she knows that order is in there somewhere and is challenged by the process. She sees not only the items that she must complete, but also the *consequences* of events under her control. And she acts tactfully and appropriately to keep things humming.

Can a person *cultivate* this temperament if she does not already possess it? I believe it is possible for some people to do so, but not everyone.

WHAT'S YOUR FIRST INSTINCT? A QUICK QUIZ

Answer all the following questions as *honestly as you can*—and remember: There's no point in deluding yourself when it comes to settling down in a job you're going to be spending most of your waking hours performing. When you've answered each question from the choices provided and marked all your answers on a separate sheet of paper, check the answer key for your results.

1. You are coordinating a formal luncheon for your manager, a high-level corporate executive, with a major foreign dignitary and his entourage. The luncheon is taking place at an exclusive club; you have been told to handle the seating arrangements and set down the place cards yourself, because your boss has had trouble with the help at this establishment in the past. When you arrive at the site,

however, you are informed by a burly guard that only members may pass into the dining room your employer has reserved. You don't have a membership card; the guard assures you that you will not be allowed in. There are 20 minutes to go before the guests start arriving. What would you be likeliest to do?

(a). Leave the seating cards with the guard and ask him to pass them along to your manager when he arrives.

(b). Confidently inform the guard that he doesn't have to watch you walk into the dining room if he doesn't want to, and then stride into the room and set up the cards.

(c). Try to determine which member of the service staff is likeliest to perform the job responsibly, and delegate the task to that person.

2. It's 4:59 on Friday afternoon. Someone has forgotten to bring an important set of instructions that your manager needs in order to set up a new piece of equipment that will be used during an important out-of-town presentation. Your manager leaves first thing Monday morning and will be stopping in for a few minutes to pick up some materials from the office. What would you be most likely to do?

(a). Leave a note on your manager's desk, prominently set out where it's impossible to miss, alerting your manager to the fact that the instructions did not come through.

(b). Stay late that night—and work through the weekend, if necessary—trying to track down the instructions or develop them from scratch through trial and error.

(c). Call your manager at home before you go; leave a thorough message on the home answering machine explaining that the instructions did not arrive.

3. Your manager has received a request to speak at an industry function but has other plans. What method would you most likely use to pass along the bad news to the inviting body?

(a). Add a brief, polite handwritten note to the bottom of the letter your manager received requesting an invitation.

(b). Call or write a formal letter to explain how disappointed your manager is that it's going to be impossible to attend.

(c). Call and leave a message with the front desk that your manager won't be able to attend.

4. Three other people have had the chance to review your company's most expensive full-page advertisement of the year. Your supervisor is out of the office; it is your job to send the advertisement off to the magazine that will be running it. Which of the following three actions would you be most likely to take?

(a). Make a brief notation to yourself about who reviewed the advertisement before sending it off without looking at it.

(b). Review it yourself personally before putting it in the overnight package, and plan to add your name to those of the others who examined it for errors once you've checked it from top to bottom.

(c). Scan the advertisement quickly to see if anything leaps out at you. Then send it out.

5. Tomorrow morning your manager has an important meeting with a group of lawyers to discuss a major contract that your organization is negotiating under intense time pressure. You are alone in the office, preparing the materials necessary for the meeting, when you realize that a serious word processing mistake on the part of a temporary worker has resulted in the loss of two generations of corrections in the document that will be the focus of the meeting. Your manager has left for the day, and you know that you cannot reconstruct the extremely complex corrections on your own.

Which of the following actions would you be most likely to take?

(a). Outline in writing the principal problems and questions related to the contract as you see them, and hope your manager will be able to resolve them before the meeting begins.

(b). Call your manager at home immediately and offer to come over that night to reconstruct the document.

(c). Leave an urgent note on your manager's desk suggesting that the meeting be rescheduled until you and he can spend the one or two hours necessary to sort things out together.

6. Because of an error in your organization's shipping department, a package is missing. It contains several pieces of artwork especially commissioned for a project of your supervisor's that is nearing its deadline. An exhaustive top-to-bottom search of your facility has yielded nothing in the past 2 days, and the artist who created the work is vacationing in Sumatra. Bear in mind, you're under oath! In addressing this situation with your supervisor, what would you be most likely to do?

(a). Explain the clear case to be made against the shipping department for losing the item in the first place.

(b). Head to the library, secure a recent guide to commercial artists, select one that seems most likely to be able to reconstruct similar work in a short period of time, and prepare a cost estimate by interviewing the artist by phone.

(c). Offer to mention the need for replacement work from a new artist at the next staff meeting.

7. A recent management hire in your department has not worked out well; however, your manager has decided for the time being not to fire this person. By chance, you hear one of the unsatisfactory manager's colleagues discussing something that surprises you: rumors of an on-the-job substance abuse problem that is seriously affecting the work of the manager in question. Which of the following would most accurately reflect your response to this situation?

(a). Do nothing. It's none of your business, and there's no percentage in getting mixed up in other people's troubles.

(b). In a private moment, tactfully ask the colleague who made the remark what the source of the rumor was. Quietly report this information to your supervisor, as well as your own estimation of how likely it is that the rumor is based in fact.

(c). Immediately report the person's drug problem to your manager.

8. You have been asked by your manager to train a staff member in a procedure on the company's new computer system. The system is an expensive one that has cost a good deal of money to design and implement, and that has been delayed—much to the agony of everyone in your company—for 8 months. In the process of getting the system up and running, you encounter a computer problem that seems to have something to do with data loss in a module of the system unrelated to your training assignment. You complete the training as your manager requested, but the technical glitch reappears the next time you visit the system. What would you be most likely to do?

   (a). Ignore the error reading, since it doesn't directly affect you or anyone with whom you work.

   (b). Write your manager a memo, or inform her in person, about the problem you've encountered and its possible ramifications.

   (c). Mention your experience to a friend of yours in another department who often talks to the people who handle management information systems.

9. Your manager has been working feverishly toward the completion of an important project, and you have been putting in quite a bit of overtime at home. The morning after the very last late-night session on this project, you know, after having gotten 4½ hours of sleep, that you're not at your best, but you drop by the office anyway to pass along the completed work. You are planning to head back home to get some rest shortly afterward. There on your desk, however, is a lengthy piece of proofreading awaiting your review, and you realize that it is due today. This is something unrelated to the current project that your manager has asked you personally to complete. Your manager is not in today; the proofreading task is a week old and has had to take a back seat to the more pressing

project you have just helped to complete. How would you be most likely to react?

(a). Give it your best shot, leave the proofreading on your manager's desk, then head back home and hit the sack.

(b). Trust that your manager will understand the delay if you put off the proofreading until the next day when you're at your best, and leave a note to that effect.

(c). Call your manager at home and ask for permission to pass the project along to someone else.

10. Your manager, a government official, has left the office for the airport; he has been posted on an important diplomatic mission. After about an hour, you realize that he has left behind a vitally important series of notes he had planned to review on board. There is no possibility for fax transmission to the fleet of the airline in question. Which of the following would you be most likely to do?

(a). Draw a big red circle around your earlier written reminder (on your manager's personal calendar) that he remember to include the notes with his luggage. That way your manager, when he returns, will have no question about whether you followed through on your end.

(b). Get into a cab; use your cellular phone to contact the airline protocol officer immediately, and intimate that a crisis can be averted only if the pilot holds the plane for 10 minutes beyond its scheduled departure time—which reflects the time it will take you to dash from the terminal into the waiting plane.

(c). Place the notes in an international overnight bag and leave word with the hotel that your manager should have the notes he needs for a few minutes before his scheduled meeting.

How Did You Score?

If you selected more "a" answers than any other kind, there's a very good chance that you are the sort of person who enjoys checking things off the list and keeping them off. You may prefer to work alone rather than with others; it's possible that you often find yourself wishing for "just a little peace and quiet" so you can get your work done. I would argue that there's a strong likelihood that you may *not* be able to develop the temperament and quick, action-oriented thinking necessary for success as an executive assistant. That's not a *certainty*, mind you, but it is nevertheless a healthy probability that you are best advised to seek another position in which to make a contribution to your chosen organization. That having been said, I want to acknowledge that human beings are truly amazing organisms and that our capacity for renewal and growth is, in the final analysis, quite boundless.

If you were more likely to select "b" answers than any other variety, and if those answers honestly reflect your outlook on your working day, then you may just have what it takes. Assuming you have and/or can develop certain technical skills, you are an excellent candidate for the career track leading to the executive assistant position, because your temperament reflects a desire to get to the bottom of things, to resolve pressing problems and spot critical errors, even if doing so means taking a little more trouble or pursuing a slightly unorthodox approach.

If the "c" responses were your most common ones, you fall into the middle ground between these two extremes. Although you probably don't have, as a matter of first instinct, the temperament most likely to lead to success as an executive assistant, I would argue that you can probably *develop* it over time.

Here's a point-by-point breakdown of the principles underlying the various questions.

Question 1, although its particulars have been altered, represents an actual experience of my own (and a memorable one, I can assure you). It tests your ability to overcome external obstacles in critical situations—an ability that will be tested time and time again as you carry out your duties as an executive assistant.

Question 2 illustrates the importance of going "above and beyond the call" to deliver results for one's manager. The executive assistant's workday does not stop at 5:00 P.M. on the dot;

if that is the kind of job you want, you should find a different line of work!

Question 3 points up the necessity of displaying care, tact, courtesy, and personal attention even when—especially when!—your manager can't.

Did you catch the underlying message of Question 4? It's designed to test your sense of commitment to rooting out error, even when the situation in question is supposed, by all concerned, to be error-free. (If every situation that's *supposed* to be error-free, and that's cleared a checklist, were *actually* error-free, no airplane would ever malfunction in flight. A reliable executive assistant always looks for the mistake that's waiting to slip past, even when someone else has reviewed the material.)

Question 5 is yet another test of the "above and beyond the call of duty" instinct, and a fairly clear-cut one from the effective executive assistant's standpoint. (Please bear in mind that not only work-related issues like the ones addressed in this question, but also such crises as an executive's family emergency or a cumbersome set of vacation logistics, might also precipitate a call and/or visit to the manager's home.)

In Question 6, the issue is whether you're likely to get sidetracked by who is at fault for a problem rather than developing a creative solution yourself.

Question 7 examines your ability to put important information in context before passing it along to your manager, thereby avoiding a needless, acrimonious conflict. This is another, subtler instance of error eradication on your manager's behalf. Such processing of potentially disruptive data—not to be confused with covering up—is an essential part of the effective executive assistant's job. (How do you know that the person who started the rumor doesn't have some personal grudge against the manager in question? In the event some real-life incident gave rise to the story, how do you know that the person who saw the event identified the substance abuser correctly? How do you know the rumor didn't get started through someone's observing the manager's use of, say, insulin?)

Question 8 tests your ability to act appropriately in the face of problems that may not directly affect you. (The process of elimination should have helped you with this one. Ignoring a potentially catastrophic computer glitch is definitely not the way to go, and mentioning the problem to someone who may or may not follow up on the information you pass along is almost as bad.) You need to be sure to track the outcome.

If you gave a "b" answer to Question 9, you also know that a delay is often preferable to a hasty, brain-fuddled review of an important document that has been specifically assigned to you for a reason. Sometimes the best kind of error eradication is the kind that puts things on hold for a while.

Question 10, like Question 1, is based loosely on a real-life incident; it probes your ability to take a "think out of the box" approach to a seemingly insurmountable logistical hurdle. No one is suggesting that you cultivate outright *dishonesty* in your dealings with others when acting on your manager's behalf. A certain amount of polite and inspired *exaggeration,* however, may from time to time arise as the only measure available to you in a dire emergency. A creative, results-first approach in such matters beats a slavish adherence to procedure any day of the week. (By the way, if you seriously considered answering "a"—calling attention to your manager's failure to act on your instructions, or describing him as an ogre when things go awry, even if he is one—you should think long and hard about your suitability for the job of executive assistant.)

Now that you've taken a good look at your own current personal standing with regard to what I call the "detail and crisis" temperament, you've probably got a better idea of how likely you are to be happy and effective as an executive assistant. The suggestions and observations below may be of help to you if you want to move from a "c" outlook to a "b" outlook—one from which you can habitually work without responding resentfully to the tasks before you.

THE IMPORTANCE OF KEEPING THINGS IN PERSPECTIVE

How do you go about altering your way of looking at the world of work so that you can see it in the way that an effective executive assistant does? By ceaselessly committing yourself to the notion of putting things in their proper perspective.

A college sophomore once wrote the following letter to her parents:

Dear Mom and Dad:

I wanted to write and bring you up to date on a few things that have been happening in my life recently. First of all, I've met a marvelous new fellow; his name is Rocky, and we're planning to get married in a couple of weeks, just as soon as his divorce from his second wife comes through. Rocky's having trouble getting all the documentation for this, because the prison is still holding on to his birth certificate for some reason, even though he's been out on parole for months. What else is happening? Let's see. It's been an extremely busy time—did I mention that I lost my part-time job?—and I'm rethinking college pretty seriously. Actually, I've decided to drop out for at least the rest of this academic year, although I do feel I want to continue my college studies at some point in the future. The big news is that I think there's a good chance I may be pregnant. I'll certainly keep you posted on this, and on our wedding date. I'm still trying to decide whether I should invite the baby's father to the ceremony; it could be awkward. I'd be interested in your opinion on this point.

Mom and Dad, If you've made it this far through my letter, please accept my congratulations. Let me assure you that not one word of what I wrote you in the paragraph you just read is true. Every word is a lie. That's the good news. The bad news is that I flunked French and got a C-minus in chemistry. But when you think about it, that news isn't really the end of the world. I'm studying hard and will try to do better next time around. All my love.

Your daughter,
Janice

This story illustrates one of the most important points for anyone who hopes to succeed as an executive assistant. *Poise, perseverance, and perspective are essential.*

The ability to see things in their true light, to attach humor to situations, to maintain unshakable poise and equanimity in the face of challenge, is an absolute must in a job where so many expected and unexpected problems intersect. Poise and perseverance are what make the calm pursuit of order, and the acceptance of constant detail orientation in one's work, possible in the first place.

Today's logistical crisis may seem like the worst thing that could possibly happen, but you must keep your composure and look to the long term. Things may seem larger than they are. In the end, your ability to put worries aside and focus on the true dimensions of whatever problem presents itself may be your most important work skill.

To succeed as an executive assistant, you must remember the old adage that promulgates two vitally important rules:

1. *Don't sweat the small stuff.*
2. *It's all small stuff.*

You will be working at a job in which things *are* going to go wrong. Accept that as a given. Deadlines will be pushed, budgets will be overrun, messages will be misinterpreted, egos will be bruised. True, you're there to double-check things in order to keep them from going wrong in the first place; but you're also there to deal with the aftermath when events *do* go wrong—which they will. What personal levels of resolve, character, and farsightedness can you adopt in order to deal with problems that arise? What mental calisthenics can you perform that will allow you to think in the long term, rather than focusing on questions like "Who's to blame?" and "How can I prove that such-and-such a person made a mistake, rather than me?" If you can step back—like the distracted parents who received that unforgettable letter—and remind yourself that the world really isn't about to collapse as the result of a problem you or someone else has identified, you'll be in a much better position to react effectively when a more profound crisis *does* surface.

You will need to learn to be good to yourself. You will need to train yourself not to fly off the handle at the first instance of setback or miscommunication. If you can't learn to respond to today's catastrophe by taking a deep breath *before* reacting, there's a very good chance that you will not be as happy or as effective as you need to be on the job.

To be sure, attaining this long-term perspective is easier said than done. Part of the reason is that most of us are programmed from an early age to equate the act of "going to work" with that of "getting things done." This is a sensible enough principle, because we *do* need, of course, to think of the best way to resolve many of the problems that come across our desk. To get them finished. To cross them off the list. To either conclude them ourselves or pass them along to someone we can trust to do the job for us.

That's a helpful way of approaching *some* of the tasks you'll be facing as an executive assistant, but it will not work as the single, unvarying approach you can take to all matters large and small. That's because now more than ever this job is a special kind of job, one that has some elements you can never expect to complete, and those elements cry out for another way of dealing with work.

As part of your daily routine, you, the executive assistant, can expect to be asked to do the following:

- Develop short-term fixes for ongoing technical problems faced by others.
- Develop short-term fixes for ongoing technical problems *you* face.
- Serve as a clearinghouse for various important pieces of information about new initiatives within the organization.

- Assess new technologies the organization may wish to implement.
- Implement the new technologies the organization has embraced.

We can add to those responsibilities such diverse problem-solving duties as these:

- Help implement, monitor, and assess an endless campaign of product and service improvement.
- Provide insight and suggestions to top management on key personnel issues.
- Help your manager mend fences between rival factions in your office.
- Tactfully fend off attacks from coworkers who tend to get a little "intense" around deadline time.
- Respond, without bruising egos, to the outsiders who want your manager's time and energy.
- Help deal with insiders who want, and can't have, your manager's time and energy.
- Attempt to reconcile continuously tight schedules.
- Coordinate extracurricular or family commitments and schedules for the executive.

Any one of these tasks can be broken down into constituent parts, but none of them can honestly be considered finished at any point. And these are just some of the dozens of "ongoing" functions you're likely to deal with. For the new executive assistant, *crossing the items off the list in such a way that they stay off is impossible.*

If we think of ourselves as going to work in order to complete these tasks (and their many variations) so that we can focus instead on our "real" work (i.e., the narrow confines of our formal job description, or the specific time-sensitive jobs we've been assigned that don't fall into an "ongoing" category), then we won't be taking the proper long-term view. We won't be seeing the various aspects of our job in their true perspective. And we'll spend a great deal of our time being frustrated, because the things we will have crossed off our list will keep reappearing!

The effective executive assistant is not so much a carrier-out of tasks as an inspired, order-bringing diplomat within the organization. She accepts that the work at hand includes a variety of challenges for which there are not necessarily *solutions,* but only *adaptations.* The desire to wrap things up and cross them off the list is healthy—if it's channeled toward the proper aims. If it's assumed as an unyielding work philosophy within the confines of the job, however, this desire is likely to make you very unhappy. The effective executive assistant realizes that there are, by definition, certain aspects of the job that are never "finished"!

Once you accept this fact and maintain an open attitude, you'll be in a much better position to develop an enlightened, experienced mindset when it comes to evaluating the various emergencies that land in your lap. You must address the most recent emergency, whatever it is, with the attention it deserves, and you must act responsibly toward it. But you must also accept that its existence is not a judgment on you personally. The particular challenge you face is almost certainly part of an ongoing *series* of challenges you should not expect to vanish with enough sustained effort on your part. There will always be an emergency or an unexpected occurrence. See the challenge for what it is, and take pleasure in contributing your knowledge and expertise to both the short-term and long-term issues it may involve. With the proper perspective you'll realize that you're dealing not with an isolated example of disorder, but with a link in the chain that affects any number of other links.

Not panicking about the various challenges you face, but rather seeing them in their true context, is one of the greatest skills you can master as an executive assistant (and a key to your career growth). And this, too, is an ongoing task that you should not expect to "finish" within a particular period of time!

In my experience, that's the best advice when it comes to developing the long-term, detail-oriented mindset necessary for success as an executive assistant (and, for that matter, in any of the typical jobs that precede that position in a normal career path). Only you can judge whether this way of looking at the world is likely to become second nature to you. If you determine that it is not, you may be best advised to seek another line of work.

A FEW THOUGHTS ON MENTOR RELATIONSHIPS

Your relationship with the executive with whom you will be working should, in the best case, be a mutually enriching one in which both of you pursue goals that benefit the organization and your respective careers. As you work your way up the ladder we discussed a little earlier in the chapter, remember that it's never too early to commit yourself to a professional alliance of this kind with a senior executive. In fact, doing so is probably one of the best ways to accelerate your ascent from a Grade I to a Grade IV position. The aim is to demonstrate that you're capable of anticipating problems before they occur, of strong critical thinking, creative (and instinctive!) problem resolution, and of long-term planning. If you can turn a short-term assignment at the Grade I, II, or III level into an opportunity to demonstrate such traits to each and every manager with whom you come into contact, you stand a good chance of developing the kind of mutually advantageous professional connections from which fulfilling careers are made.

How does a mentor relationship begin? Typically, the mentor you are seeking is an Executive Assistant to an executive at a higher level. Begin by asking for insight and feedback in a particular area. As you undertake these tactful, unstated "auditions" for potential mentors at the early stages of your career, don't forget that the junior partner in a mentor relationship is just that—a junior partner. Let the person with whom you're working know that you are eager to benefit from his or her experience. Maintain an open mind. See mistake correction as an aspect of mentorship. Fulfill all duties you are assigned completely and conscientiously. Do research. Know what you don't know, and ask about how to proceed. Make a habit of going the extra mile for your potential mentor; then make it clear that you appreciate the opportunity to learn and to grow professionally as a result of your work with this person.

SOME FINAL THOUGHTS BEFORE WE MOVE ON TO THE JOB SEARCH

You say you're ready to start making contacts and working your way toward an executive assistant position? You'll find a detailed battle plan for your job search in the next chapter. Before you start making calls, however, bear in mind this chapter's advice on the likely career path you'll face, the broad keys for success within the job, and the personal temperament you will need to either possess or cultivate as you begin to develop professional contacts in this area. The points you've just read will help you to craft the message you'll be sending to prospective employers!

And remember: You're asking to work in a position whose very description may well be subject to constant change! You accept—make that "relish"—special challenges, especially unfamiliar ones!

CHAPTER TWO

A BRIEF OVERVIEW OF TODAY'S SUCCESSFUL JOB SEARCH

Life shrinks or expands in proportion to one's courage.

—ANAIS NIN

There is no single right way to get a job as an executive assistant, but there is a combination of methods you can use to develop leads and extend your contact network. In this chapter, we'll look at those methods, help you develop your interview strategy, and talk a little about a number of other steps you can take to land the right job offer.

Before we begin talking about what you *should* do as part of your job search campaign, though, let's isolate a few things that you *shouldn't* if you decide to do it all on your own:

- *Don't* focus all your efforts on a single promising lead. The successful job search has been cogently described as a long series of no's leading to a single yes; your aim is to get all the no's out of the way so you can talk to the people most likely to consider hiring you, and you can't do that if you're spending 1 or 2 weeks in a row obsessing about a single prospective employer. Job searching is a numbers game; to make it work, you must continuously develop lots of *new* contacts, and you must do so as a matter of course.
- *Don't* take rejection personally. A decision maker's choice not to offer you a position *today* is not a judgment on you as a person; acting as though it is will only leave you less well prepared to showcase your talents, aptitudes, and enthusiasm for

the next prospective employer. However, it may be worthwhile to ask for the reasons you were not offered the position.

- *Don't* be rude or assume a defensive posture to any representative of the target organization, for any reason. You will only do yourself a disservice by displaying anything other than unshakable politeness to anyone who works for the target company, whether or not that person has any contact with the final decision maker. Consider yourself to be "on stage" at all times, during the interview or at any other point you come in contact with the organization. Too many candidates have lost job offers that should have been theirs by making thoughtless remarks (such as revealing private information about your previous employer) while the company considered their candidacy. Don't be one of them.
- *Don't* be afraid to contact more than one person within a company. The personnel office may be able to point you toward the right opening; then again, contacting an executive directly has yet to be construed by the Supreme Court as a violation of the United States Constitution.
- *Don't* misspell or mispronounce people's names. Call ahead and confirm the proper spellings and pronunciations of even simple-sounding names. Getting someone's name wrong shows a lack of attention to detail and is the surest way to make someone tune out the rest of your message.
- *Don't* pass along any written document—résumé, cover letter, or any other element of your job search that takes the form of words on paper—unless it has been proofread by you over and over again, and then scrutinized closely *by someone else.* Today's computerized spell-checkers are both a blessing and a curse. They spot egregious spelling mistakes ("to apply" spelled as "tto apply," for instance), but they pass in silence over spelling errors that happen to reflect real words in the dictionary ("to apply" spelled as "too apply.") Such tools are extraordinarily dangerous, because they give us a false sense of security! You are applying for a job in which spelling and grammatical skills are of the highest importance. A good percentage of the people who will be reading what you pass

along—probably a clear majority—will reject your candidacy instantly if they spot a single spelling or typographical error. We do at The Duncan Group. Don't risk that. Find a friend who can assist you by reviewing all your job-search documents and helping you to make them absolutely error-free.

- *Don't* procrastinate. Looking for a job *is* a job, and it should be treated as such. Your aim is to display in this effort the same perseverance, diligence, promptness, courtesy, organization, and attention to detail you would in the office where you wish to work. During the hours you set aside for your job-search efforts, turn off the television, put away the magazine you've been reading, and get down to business. Some people decide that the best way to focus their efforts when it comes to getting work done on the "job-search job" is to transfer their research or contact efforts to someplace other than their home: a library, say, or a friend's house that has been vacated during business hours. Others get up at an early hour to write contact letters and prepare them for mailing, or make special child-care arrangements during the precious hours available to call prospective employers. Still others grant themselves appropriate rewards (a desired recording, perhaps, or a luscious snack) once a session has been completed. If you need to employ these self-motivating techniques in order to devote a solid 7 to 9 focused hours per day to your job search, so be it. But *don't* get distracted by personal calls, your favorite Internet trivia site, or anything else during the time you have allotted for employment networking efforts.
- *Don't* come off as arrogant or overbearing in your contacts with people within the target organization. You are applying for a sensitive position, one in which tact and the ability to work well with people matter a great deal. It *is* possible to be persistent without being obnoxious. Make sure you're on the right side of that line.
- *Don't* speak ill of your present, or any previous, employer. The people who will be considering hiring you will almost certainly know nothing about your skills and background. In order to fill that knowledge gap, they will be listening for sto-

ries from your past that will illuminate the type of employee you're likely to be. Even if you were completely in the right and an incompetent supervisor was completely in the wrong, a prospective employer is likely to presume that *any* communication problems you describe represent *your* inability to make a situation work. Let's face it: Managers tend to side with managers in these situations. If you share confidential information about a previous employer, the interviewer will very likely conclude that you lack the discretion so essential to the executive assistant's role.

Accentuate the positive in all your previous positions. When you must describe serious problems in your work history, emphasize what you learned from the situation without going into great detail, and point out how you were able to help others from making costly mistakes.

- *Don't* exaggerate your accomplishments. Doing so is a serious career risk, engaged in only by the foolhardy. Make sure all your written and spoken representations are truthful; do not claim to have attained any educational honors that you have not, and do not claim to have worked anywhere that you did not. These days, employers are likely not only to fire but to consider suing employees who get themselves hired under false pretenses. Make sure your hire and termination dates are accurate. Don't falsify information on your résumé.
- *Don't* neglect your personal appearance. You are applying for a position that will almost certainly require you to serve as the representative of your company and your manager to some very important people. How you look matters. Keep your dress conservative; be sure your grooming and hygiene are impeccable. When in doubt, come across as *more* formal-looking than necessary. Do not opt for excessive jewelry, inappropriate cosmetics, or overwhelming perfume. These mistakes often form devastating, negative first impressions that lose jobs.
- *Don't* say you'll "do anything." Yes, you must present yourself as a generalist, the type of employee who can master a good many systems in a short period of time. But that's not the same thing as yielding control of your lifetime work goals to someone else. You must place the responsibility for focusing

your energy and intelligence on the prospective employer, because today's employers are, for the most part, looking for people who *make things make sense,* not people who wait for instructions or have no idea how to deal with challenging situations. This is perhaps truer for the executive assistant than for anyone else in the organization! The person who is considering hiring you is in all likelihood on the lookout for an executive assistant who has a strong sense of purpose. Saying you'll "do anything," or coming off as despairing, doesn't send that purposeful message! *Specify* what you're good at and *why* you're good at it, and identify the matches you see between your skills and the target company's needs.

"HOW DO I GET IN TOUCH WITH THE PEOPLE WHO CAN HIRE ME?"

Actually, there are as many answers to this question as there are hiring officials. Start by remembering that each person you contact is an individual, and each organization demands both a certain amount of research and a *customized* résumé and cover letter based on that research. With those principles as your starting point, you can pursue any number of techniques in order to secure a job offer as an executive assistant. About the only real mistake you can make is to focus exclusively on a *single* method—and this is certainly a common enough error. Many job seekers decide to look by simply focusing on one method of learning about openings (usually classified advertisements). You must generate as many leads as possible, and you must vary your approach by incorporating a *number* of tactics for tracking down openings. Remember: *Focusing on the result of a single job-search query, rather than developing a broad network of contacts, is what makes for long job searches.* Contact many prospective employers and follow up appropriately with each. You should, of course, be prepared to discuss such issues as your past achievements and innovations, special projects you've worked on, your clerical skill levels, software proficiency, and any other relevant aspects of your professional experience.

Here's a brief review of some of the most popular methods for contacting employers. You should strongly consider incorporating *at least five* of these methods into your search.

Contacting the Company's Personnel or Human Resources Office. Many job-search experts suggest that you avoid human resources people on the theory that since these officials are not the true decision makers, they (1) don't grasp the extent of the executive assistant's role, (2) rarely know the subtle requirements of top decision makers (such as CEOs) personally, and (3) spend most of their time rejecting people. There is something to be said for these assertions, but it's also true that you may be shunted toward human resources anyway. If you do try to contact the company through this route, you must try like the dickens to track down a formal, written job description and build your résumé and cover letter around the points of contact between your background and that description (provided it is factual). By developing a résumé that features nothing but direct matches with the formal description, you're more likely to make the first cut and have your résumé passed on to another person within the organization. Displaying your poise, charm, and tactful persistence on the telephone before and after you send in the résumé and cover letter probably won't hurt your cause, either.

Personnel and human resources officials tend to take a long time to respond. This is certainly one reason to avoid building your job search entirely upon the personnel approach.

Contacting an Executive in Need of an Executive Assistant. Contacting a hiring executive is a great opportunity, although hard to come by unless you happen to be hooked into a company's network. Don't be afraid to deal directly with a top-level official in this category. Use voicemail to your advantage.

Telling All Your Acquaintances About the Type of Work You're Seeking. Strongly recommended! Remember, you are now in a "marketing mode." The more people who know about your employment objective, the better off you're likely to be. It's easier to talk with current acquaintances about your job search than complete strangers, right? So tell friends and family, appropriate colleagues, attorneys, accountants, doctors, and anyone in the business community you happen to know about the job you're trying to land. Ask for their help in passing along leads.

Consulting Classified Advertisements. Want-ads may be worth spending some time on, but not too much! Competition for advertised openings is often quite fierce. You stand a better statistical chance of landing the executive assistant position you're after by contacting a company directly. If you spend more than 25 percent of your available time pursuing classified openings, there's a very strong likelihood that you are neglecting other methods that could help you find the job you deserve more quickly. And beware: Answering a blind ad may put you in the potentially uncomfortable position of unwittingly applying for a job at your current employer!

Working with an Executive Search Firm. The Duncan Group is the only such firm that operates on a search basis for retained executive assistant positions.

Writing Letters to Top Executives. I highly recommend a letter-writing campaign. It is not, perhaps, the highest-percentage gambit on the list—face-to-face contact building probably presents a better batting average—but then again, you're after only one job offer, and this has been known to pay off very good dividends. How much work does it take to put together 20 or 30 prospective names at the library? Your best bet is to develop a letter that's a little unusual, one that incorporates some appropriate humor. In crafting this letter—indeed, in preparing any employment appeal for this position—remember that one of your chief selling points is your ability to *fill the prospective employer's gaps:* to do well that which he or she doesn't do well or has no inclination to do well. The more specific the letter is to the demands of the recipient's industry or company, the more likely you are to win the kind of attention you're after. Keep your letter to a single page. Follow up by telephone.

Forming an Alliance with Working Executive Assistants. Developing a friendly network of executive assistants willing to keep an eye out for opportunities that could be right for you is one of the best ways to find out about job openings before the rest of the world does. Don't be afraid to appeal to someone directly by saying something along the lines of, "I want to ask your help: What advice would you offer someone who's seeking a position as an executive assistant? Do you know of any openings I should be pursuing?" Here is where it is beneficial to seek out organizations and advocacy groups that support the role of the Executive Assistant.

Personal Ads Find Relationships, Why Not Emloyees? Write an interesting advertisement about your talents, achievements, personal values, and the level of position you seek and strategically place in publications read by the industry of your choice. This works!

Asking for Help on Your Résumé. When you run into someone who has the power to move your candidacy forward, it's always a good idea to ask, pleasantly and tactfully, for help in assessing your (already customized) résumé—at his or her convenience, of course. This is a subtle, nonintrusive way to secure valuable input and build allies within the organization, and it doesn't force your contact to feel as though he or she has betrayed you if a job offer is not immediately forthcoming. Rest assured, however, that more than one person has secured an offer through this inventive method of winning "buy-in" from a contact. It's worth repeating: The more carefully crafted your résumé is to the particular requirements of the person for whom you'll be working, the better off you'll be.

Attending Seminars, Meetings, and Industry Conventions. In other words, hunt down the executives where they gather—without their gatekeepers. If you can approach them one on one during scheduled breaks, and before and after the program, you will almost certainly be able to uncover some good leads.

Remember, you're not only looking for people who don't currently have an assistant; you're also looking for people who are *currently dissatisfied* with the help they're receiving. Fortunately for you, this is a rather large percentage of the total pool of executives! Develop a natural-sounding professional introduction. If you follow this approach persistently and courteously, make plenty of eye contact, and keep a supply of personal cards bearing your contact information handy at all times, you'll walk away with more leads than you started out with, and that's the name of the game. A strong word of advice: be absolutely professional in your approach so that your "profession" is not mistaken!

Securing a Temporary Position, then Trying to Parlay It into a Long-Term Job. Temping has worked for many people. There is, after all, no better "interview" than a sterling piece of on-the-job accomplishment. The technique should probably be something you keep in the back of your mind during a temporary assignment you'd be working anyway, rather than an effort undertaken specifically to land a particular job. There are too many variables beyond your control for you to spend all day trying to track down the perfect temp assignment, and your time is probably the most important resource during your job search.

Whichever combination of methods you choose, make sure you send the right messages as you put them to work. You are confident, but not overbearing; you are a self-starter, but you never lose sight of team goals. You are well groomed and well spoken. You understand the importance of policies and procedures, but you don't wait around for permission to address pressing problems that look like they're about to become a lot worse. You are tactful. You don't tell tales out of school. You don't collapse when someone points out a mistake. You deal well with fellow employees at all levels. You know how to make someone else look good, and doing so gives you a certain satisfaction.

YOUR RÉSUMÉ

As I've stated above, the best résumé is one that is specifically targeted to a particular opening. Your résumé should use *internal* information from the target organization to develop a number of compelling points provided it accurately reflects your work experience. Ideally, there should be no point on your résumé that doesn't match up with something you *know* the prospective employer to be seeking.

I don't believe there is any one perfect résumé that will magically secure the interest of the hiring official, but I do believe there are variations that can profitably serve as inspiration as you uniquely develop your own on the basis of information you've gathered during your research. Here are some examples that may help to get you started.

Jane Smith
123 Main St.
Anytown NY 00000
Business: 212/555-1212
Residence: 212/555-1213

Summary of Qualifications

Accomplished and innovative administrative assistant with twenty years of executive secretarial experience in the legal and investment banking fields. Highly motivated. Persuasive writing abilities. Analytical and research-oriented with excellent computer skills.

Work Experience

1993–Present Management Corporation
Anytown, NY

Administrative Associate to the founding partner of a private investment partnership directing an equity fund of over $680 million. Responsibilities include all corporate and personal correspondence as well as the review and processing of legal documents. Managed several estate properties and extensive art collection, working closely with attorneys, architects and curators. Organized complicated domestic and international travel itineraries and schedules, supervising private jet staff and related support personnel. Served as social secretary, planning and executing private dinner parties and benefits for charitable interests.

1987–1993 Anytown Transit Police Benevolent Association
Anytown, NY

	Executive Assistant to the president of the transit police union. Office manager responsible for all aspects of day-to-day operations of the office, supervising clerical/secretarial staff of eight. Developed and instituted general office automation as well as successfully completed total renovation of offices.
1976–1986	Adams Perfumes, Inc. *Anytown, NY*
	Executive secretary to president and office manager.
	Education Ashleywilde College *Anytown, NY* Bachelor of Arts, English (1997) Dean's List Friends of the Ashleywilde Fellowship
	Ellen Biggs School *Anytown, NY* Secretarial Diploma, 1978
	Accreditation
	Notary Public

(*Continued*)

Jane Smith
123 Main St.
Anytown, NY 00000
212/555-1212

PROFESSIONAL EXPERIENCE

November 1994–Present

SMITH & JONES HOLDINGS INC.
Scheduling Assistant and Executive Secretary to Chairman
Work closely with Chairman to assure his comfort and knowledge of all corporate and personal scheduling matters. Responsible for all details of intricate daily, weekend, yearly calendars. Liaison between Chairman's office and Chief of Staff, Vice Presidents, wife's office, bodyguards, limousine drivers, flight crews, chefs, nannies, household staffs, interior decorators. Prepare traveling bags with current detailed files, medications, relevant meeting back-up. Present daily invitations and contribution requests. Screen countless phone calls to office. Manage all corporate files. Sole support staff to Chairman for entire weekend twice a month.

March 1993–September 1994

KAZILAK SERVICES, INC.
Executive Assistant to Chairman
Managed tight and fluctuating daily schedule. Assembled preparation materials for corporate meetings including board, chairman's staff, and shareholders' meetings. Orchestrated business and personal itineraries working with chauffeurs, pilots of corporate plane, helicopter broker, travel agent, and various concierges. Implemented crucial follow-up lists, i.e., calls to return, meetings to be scheduled, reminders. Oversaw current personal and business files. Maintained high level of confidentiality during merger negotiations with ABC, Inc., organizational restructuring, chairman's resignation. Presided over office relocation to ABC, Inc. and subsequently to ALL-WAY. Assisted in coordination of major renovation work to corporate apartment. Supervised corporate apartment housekeeper and scheduled decorator, landscaping, and maintenance appointments.

November 1987–February 1993

MASSWAY DEVELOPMENT
Administrative Assistant to President
Acted as liaison between construction managers, engineers, architects and Borough officials. Coordinated and presided over office relocation. Designed extensive file system. Supervised luncheons and receptions for directors and associates. Reconciled two bank accounts daily. Maintained personal portfolio files. Assisted in investigation of commercial development sites.

MYRON & RICHARD PARTNERS
Administrative Assistant to Law Firm Senior Partner
Communicated daily with clients, attorneys, investment bankers and corporate executives. Developed, implemented and maintained accounting system. Scheduled meetings, conferences and real estate closings. Responded to inquiries and composed correspondence. Provided dependable, organized support system to employer and associates.

SKILLS

Computer:	Microsoft Word, Word for Windows, WordPerfect 5.1, Spreadsheet
Typing:	70 WPM
Shorthand:	80–90 WPM

EDUCATION

Overton State College
Candidate for B.S. 1992–Present

Ellen Biggs School
Certified Graduate, Secretarial Program 1985

(*Continued*)

Jane Smith
123 Main St.
Anytown, NY 00000
(h) 212/555-1212; (o) 212/555-1213

EXPERIENCE

4/89 to present

Executive Secretary to a Financial Executive in following positions

Jones Securities Inc., New York, NY
Executive Secretary to CEO

Global emerging markets investment banking firm established June 1995 (staff of nine has expanded to sixty-one). Performed most administrative functions during the initial stage of setting up the New York office. Organized rentals of office furniture for temporary space, purchased supplies, telephone, office equipment and established vendor relationships, assisted CFO with broker/dealer registration and accounts payable, liaison with technology consultants. Current administrative responsibilities include interviewing applicants for support staff positions, managing the group insurance plans, maintaining employee files, acting as the contact person for the group travel agency account, corporate memberships, building management office, and coordination of corporate apartments. Provide secretarial support to CEO as well as the Chairman and other overseas executives visiting New York office. [6/95 to Present]

Securities International, Inc., New York, NY
Executive Secretary to Executive Vice President

Performed secretarial duties for Executive Committee Member responsible for the research-driven Equity Division. In 1994 took on the responsibility for arranging luncheons and conferences presenting company management to investors. This involved contact with Investor Relations staff, company public relations departments, hotel catering staff, and institutional clients. Wrote introductory speeches for management hosting these functions. Acted as liaison with ABC Technology to restructure the master client mailing list. General administrative duties for Equity Division. [5/93 to 6/95]

Globe Corporation, New York, NY
Executive Secretary to Vice Chairman

Performed secretarial duties for Vice Chairman, who had responsibility for marketing the firm's investment products to international investors and establishing international strategic alliances. Maintained his personal and business calendars, screened calls, took dictation, set up senior level meetings, approved expenditures for department. Acted as liaison with marketing consultants. Also organized Vice Chairman's schedule at the annual World Technology Forum in Bonn, Germany and the firm's reception at the meeting. Arranged his international travel itineraries, which entailed contact with the management of European and Asian firms. Served as the contact person for his outside board membership activities and in this capacity helped organize and attended several fundraising functions. [4/89 to 5/93]

(*Continued*)

1/82 to 4/85	Word Processing Service, Anytown, NY *Self employed* Provided typing and editorial services to Anytown University students, attorneys in private practice, a marketing consultant, and other small downtown businesses.
EDUCATION	
	University of Anytown, Bachelor of Science degree in Anthropology, 1988 University of Anytown, undergraduate courses in Business Administration
INTERESTS	
	People, art, literature, travel.
SKILLS	
	Type 70 wpm, fast longhand. Proficient in Microsoft Word for Windows, ACT, Excel.

(*Continued*)

Jane Smith
123 Main St.
Anytown, NY 00000
Home: (212) 555-1212
Office: (212) 555-1213

4/90 to Present: POWELL MANAGEMENT CONSULTING

Office Manager

International management consulting firm. The firm provides management consulting services to Fortune 200 companies in the areas of Financial Services, Transportation, Telecommunications, Marketing, and General Strategy.

Responsible for management of an office of 100 + employees. Duties include support hiring, training, and supervision of an administrative staff of 20, budget preparation (includes staffing needs forecasting), human resources coordination (benefits, payroll, schedules, orientation, and training), facilities management (office operations/maintenance, purchasing, accounts payable approval and processing, telecommunications, office furniture and equipment purchasing, and lease negotiation), events planning and coordination, vendor negotiation, as well as all other details relevant to maintaining smooth office flow.

7/86 to 3/90 PARKER & BUSH

Administrative Assistant
Managing Partner and Operations Partner

Assistant to a Managing Partner of a full service, international accounting firm

	(providing service in the areas of Mergers & Acquisitions, Bankruptcy, Business Consulting, Real Estate, etc.).
	Organize day in terms of schedule and commitments to clients, staff, and office management. Provide administrative and secretarial support to include the preparation of business and personal correspondence, agenda and meeting coordination, preparation of meeting minutes, liaise with personal attorneys, bankers, realtors and investment brokers, as well as the management of a support secretary.
1983 to 1986	SMITH SURGICAL *Secretary* *Three physician surgical practice*
	Responsibilities included schedule coordination, transcription of medical records/notes, insurance administration (thorough knowledge of third party reimbursement/appeals), etc.
Education:	State University of Anytown Business Administration (Management), 1982 Heavy concentration on Accounting/Finance/Supervision courses.
Office Skills:	Knowledge of Macintosh and IBM computers; software includes: Multimate, Multimate Advantage, DW3 & DW4, Microsoft Word, Wang, NBI, and WordPerfect 5.1, MacDraw, Persuasion, Ready Set Show, Microsoft Excel, and Lotus 1-2-3. Gregg Shorthand: 90 wpm

(*Continued*)

Jane Smith
123 Main Street, Anytown, NY 00000
212/555-1212

OBJECTIVE:

To contribute to the success of a growth-oriented company in an administrative support position with diverse responsibilities.

PROFILE:

A strong self-starter with more than 15 years of increasingly responsible administrative experience working for senior level management in a variety of industries. Adaptive, competent, problem solver highly responsive to challenging situations. Effective at meeting deadlines and working under pressure. Excellent communication and planning skills with attention to detail. Commitment to performance excellence. Microsoft Word, WordPerfect, Lotus, and Excel for Windows; stenography. Notary Public, State of New Jersey.

PROFESSIONAL EXPERIENCE:

MARTIN DIRECT MARKETING, INC. 1993 to Present

Administrative Assistant to the President
Provide administrative support to the President and Chief Financial Officer in the company's New Jersey and New York offices. Coordinate responsibilities and administrative functions in each location.

- Developed and implemented procedures to facilitate communication among senior level staff at six nationally located offices increasing daily productivity.
- Prepared daily finance reports for staff to track shipments/revenue.

- Organized quarterly companywide conferences for senior level executives; negotiated conference rates; coordinated travel; planned meals/banquets/meetings; organized extracurricular activities.
- Resolved customer complaints directed to the President, improving customer retention.

ABC GROUP 1992 to 1993

Executive Assistant to the President
Assisted the President, Chairman, and Board of Directors with all executive duties and provided administrative support on large commercial loan matters. Maintained confidential client and bank files.

- Assisted in preparation of monthly and quarterly asset review and loan classification reports for Board meetings; prepared formal Board meeting minutes.
- Scheduled monthly departmental and Board meetings insuring quorum.
- Prepared and processed, from complaint to writ of execution, legal documents associated with foreclosures for in-house counsel.
- Resolved customer complaints directed to the President improving customer satisfaction.

NEWTON ASSOCIATES, Inc. 1986 to 1993

Office Manager
Monitored all month, quarter, and year-end sales tax and payroll reporting, sales data and analyses, as well as general secretarial duties for $10 + million retail business. Directed duties of assistant.

TECHWARE, INC. 1985 to 1986

Secretary/Salaried Personnel
Assisted Personnel Director with recruiting, annual reviews, and medical benefit management for salaried employees. Assumed department responsibilities when Director was promoted to Chicago Division.

(*Continued*)

EDUCATION:

WHITE BUSINESS SCHOOL - Anytown, NY
Graduate, 1983

SPECIAL TRAINING:

Various computer courses at Anytown Community College, Anytown, NY, and Personal Computer Skills Center, Bigtown, NY, 1984.

(*Continued*)

Jane Smith
123 Main St.
Anytown, NY 00000
212/555-1212

SUMMARY

OFFICE MANAGER with extensive and diversified experience in managing start-ups and on-going operations. Related areas of expertise include:

Purchasing/Negotiating
Relocation/Space Planning
Computer Systems
Cost Control
Payroll & Accounts Payable
Telecommunications
Maintenance Services
Human Resources/Benefits
Office Equipment

EXPERIENCE

1994–1996 McCarter Investments, New York, NY
Money Managers, Private Investment Firm, Trading Operations.

Office Manager - Responsible for the overall day-to-day operations of the Company, including all telecommunications and on-line services for the trading floor. Analyzed, negotiated, and purchased all office equipment, supplies, and outside services. Responsible for all phases of a recent and on-going relocation of the office due to merger. Prior move included responsibility for scheduling, planning, reviewing floor plans, solicitation of contractor bids, construction, lighting, security systems, etc. Supervision of support staff.

Acting Human Resource/Payroll Manager - Concurrent responsibilities included implementation and administration of employee benefits programs, corporate insurance, and 401K plan for over 350 employees including active, inactive, and domestic employees at multiple locations. Responsible for interviewing, hiring, and firing employees. Responsible for the management and administration of three payrolls and employee taxes. Maintained payroll systems, tax records, and personnel records.

Administrative Assistant/Accounts Payable to the CFO - Financial responsibilities included reviewing all invoices and expenditures. Responsible for accounts payable, money market, and payroll accounts. Calculations for year-end and on-going monthly evaluations. Handled administration and follow-up on wire transfers. Handled all aspects of assisting the Chief Financial Officer including travel and scheduling. Set up filing systems.

1991–1994 ABC SERVICES, Secaucus, NJ
Private Money Management Firm and Services Organization.

Office Manager/Assistant to CFO - Responsible for managing the office including office facilities and services, personnel and benefits, and administrative functions. Negotiated, analyzed, and selected suppliers, contractors, vendors, and brokers. Approved all expenditures and cost cutting, maintained all office, telecommunications, and computer equipment. Oversaw office relocation including space planning. Personnel responsibilities included benefit analyses and administration, hiring and supervising staff. Responsible for payroll and salary administration.

1989–1991 UNIVERSAL INFORMATION SERVICES, New York, NY
SEC Division of Engineering Firm.

Office and Operations Manager - Responsible for the supervision and management of the entire office. Responsibilities included ordering of equipment and supplies, negotiating contracts, and financial duties. Human resource functions included staffing, interviewing, hiring, firing, and performance reviews. Analyzed operations procedures. Handled arrangements for travel, training programs, and trade shows.

(Continued)

1988–1989 THE SAXWAY COMPANY, Stamford, CT (Bankrupt) Manufacturing Firm.

Office Manager - Responsible for running operations of office and supervised staff. Wrote presentations, reports, and correspondence. Participated in Board Meetings. Liaison between clients, public relations firms, and advertising agencies. Preparation for and participation in trade shows. Set up computer library.

Began career as Assistant to Vice President, Systems, Marywood International in New York, NY. Contributed to design and layout of modular office furniture and lighting, 1987.

EDUCATION

Post College, Anytown, NY
Ellen Biggs, Anytown, NY

SKILLS

Knowledge of computer software programs (Microsoft Word, Microsoft Excel, Microsoft Money, Power Point, WordPerfect, Lotus, Harvard Graphics), all office equipment (computer hardware, faxes, copiers, postage machines, etc.), and communications equipment.

REFERENCES

Available upon request.

(*Continued*)

COVER LETTERS

Never send a résumé without a cover letter. Leaving out the cover letter is rude and counterproductive, and it's also a missed opportunity.

Your cover letter should be brief, to the point, and memorable. Most of the cover letters prospective employers receive are deadly dull; use this fact to your advantage. Take the time to develop a letter that uses appropriate language to make a few key points that will land your résumé in the "keep" pile.

Some examples of strong cover letters follow. Don't try to imitate them word for word; use them to develop unique, short summaries of your own strong suits that make people want to read (and hear) more about you.

Note: These are cover letters based on composites of actual letters we have received at The Duncan Group over the years. Although these letters are targeted to a search firm, you may use them as models for contacting a variety of organizations and adapt them to your own needs.

555 NW 17th St.
Acorn, NE 65666

October 1, 19XX

Attn: Vera
Fax (212) 555-1163

I wish to be considered for Executive Assistant positions your firm may be seeking to fill on behalf of its clients. My preference is for a position in a major media corporation or a company with an international orientation. My minimum salary expectation is $60,000.

As you will note in the following résumé, my experience and interests are in working as a "right hand man" to senior individuals, carrying substantial responsibilities, rather than in positions which are predominantly secretarial in nature.

My recent background is in working for senior motion-picture company executives, including the head of Very Large Hits, Incorporated. I assisted the president of this organization in day-to-day operations, including the administration of a considerable budget as well as in his responsibilities as Chief Executive Officer. During my time in the motion picture industry (1982–1992) I worked regularly with senior executives monitoring world media and news events, and briefing them regarding areas of risk and opportunity.

I am well organized, detail oriented, and capable of handling complicated and confidential matters effectively. I have extensive research and writing experience and have published numerous business and academic articles.

I plan to relocate to the Anytown area in December. However, if an attractive position became available, I could relocate at an earlier date. As my wife already works in Anytown, I will be making frequent visits. My next planned trip is for the period

October 11th to 18th, although these dates could be adjusted if required.

Many thanks for your time and attention.

Sincerely yours,

Brian Acata

Office (908) 555-1212
Home (908) 555-1213

____

(*Continued*)

Ellen Fialkow
60 Meadowbrook Road
Anytown, NY 10011

November 1, 19XX

TO: Barbara Versifa (via fax 212-555-1163)
REGARDING: Executive Assistant Position

Dear Barbara:

"IT CAN'T BE DONE—GIVE IT TO ELLEN!"

Faith Erin suggested I contact you regarding job opportunities you might currently be seeking to fill. Attached for your consideration are my résumé and references.

The position of Executive Assistant to a senior executive requires a diverse range of skills. I have a high level of competence and value to contribute in this role. In addition to the necessary administrative skills—encompassing organizational matters, writing projects, and computer-related tasks—I have an unusual background that helps me accomplish the supposedly "undoable."

I've worked with some top-flight people in industries ranging from investment banking to medical instrumentation. I care deeply about people and I am eager to help them achieve the most they possibly can.

I like working as an executive assistant. It provides me with the opportunity to apply all I've learned over a long working career.

Barbara, I'm seeking a position that's the "right fit," as I want to work in this position until retirement. Please keep me in mind regarding positions for which you believe I might be well suited. I look forward to speaking with you soon.

Sincerely,

Ellen Fialkow

(*Continued*)

Karen Fallows-Freeman
201 East 17th Street, Apt. 6F
Anytown, NY 10021
212/555-1212 (h)
212/555-1213 (w)

October 1, 19XX

Ms. Tracy Freedson
Corporate Solutions
143 Mason Avenue
9th Floor
Anytown, NY 10017

Dear Ms. Freedson:

I am writing at the suggestion of Dierdre McMann and Maureen Eiverson, both of whom spoke very highly of you and your search firm. I have spent over 20 years working closely with some very prominent international, civic, and business leaders, and I am presently seeking new employment opportunities. The skills, experience, and background my candidacy represents are, I believe, highly marketable.

Some history: I came to my present position as Special Assistant to the Chairman of the American Conference nearly three years ago at the invitation of Dierdre McMann, with whom I had worked closely for more than twelve years. When the opportunity arose to join her at the Conference a few months into her tenure as Chairwoman of that organization, I was excited by the prospect of continuing what had proved to be an effective partnership in public service, this time in the independent sector.

Upon Dierdre's departure last May for her present post as President of Anytown State University, I agreed to remain with the Conference during the transition period to assure continuity for the national executive office during the search for Dierdre's successor. That search is nearing its conclusion, and now is an appropriate time for me to explore professional employment options outside the organization.

I look forward to hearing from you. Please feel free to call me at either my office or at home. Many thanks!

Sincerely,

Karen Fallows-Freeman

Enclosure (résumé)

(*Continued*)

Ms. Michelle Beattie
Corporate Solutions
143 Mason Avenue
9th Floor
Anytown, NY 10017

October 1, 19XX

Dear Ms. Beattie:

I am interested in pursuing employment opportunities as an executive assistant. The enclosed résumé will furnish you with the specific details of my work background.

May I ask that we meet at your earliest convenience? I'm eager to discuss your reactions to my résumé—and to talk about the significant contributions I could make on the job.

Sincerely,

Karen O'Malley
212/555-1212 (h)
212/555-1213 (w)

Frances Baynes
327 Smith Street
Anytown, NY 10011

Michelle Beattie
Corporate Solutions
143 Mason Avenue
9th Floor
Anytown, NY 10017

October 1, 19XX

Dear Ms. Baynes:

With over nine years as an Executive Assistant/Manager in the software industry, I believe I can handle almost any situation. I invite you to look over my résumé and take note of the many duties and responsibilities that have come my way over the years.

I believe I have developed a good business sense, high levels of personal efficiency, and a strong sense of humor. Even though my career has been based in the software field for the past nine years, the skills I've developed in that time leave me in an excellent position to cross over into virtually any industry. Let me offer one example of my flexibility: After six years of acting as the CEO's "right hand," I was transferred to the London distribution office of Cerex Software on a one-year assignment to assist in the marketing and distribution of all Cerex products throughout England.

The position I'm looking for is likely to be as an assistant to a key executive at a Fortune 500 organization. I hope we can get together to talk about professional opportunities in the very near future.

Sincerely,

Frances Baynes
327 Smith Street
Anytown, NY 10011
212/555-1212 (h); 212/555-1213 (w)

____

(*Continued*)

THE INTERVIEW

They want to talk to you! Congratulations. A few cautions:

- Avoid, if at all possible, any variation on the telephone interview. I realize that it is often very difficult to change the mind of a hiring official who has decided that a phone interview is in order, and certainly there are times when you will have no choice but to submit to this. But in those cases where you *can* propose a face-to-face meeting in a briskly confident, upbeat way, you certainly should. The reason? Telephone interviews are almost always designed to be briefer and less open-ended than personal interviews. They are intended primarily to winnow out unattractive or inappropriate candidates. You simply won't have the chance to shine in quite the same way that you would during an in-person interview; your physical presence across from the interviewer will make you more tangible, more *human.* A voice on the other end of the line, however, is fairly easy to forget and/or reject. Put more succinctly, there's probably no way you can win the job offer over the phone. Strive to win a face-to-face meeting if you can.
- Make sure you look and feel your best for a personal interview. Give due care and attention to matters of dress, grooming, and personal hygiene. Be sure you are well rested; do not attempt to cram for the interview by staying up late the night before, preparing for questions that may come your way. If you have to choose between practicing answers and getting the rest you need, choose sleep.
- Show up *early.* Get a detailed, reliable set of directions to the place where you'll be interviewing. If you have the time, *practice getting there ahead of time.* If you get lost on the way to the interview site, you'll not only make a poor impression, but will probably come across as rather frenzied when you walk in the door.

- Bring extra copies of your tailored résumé, along with extra copies of any reference letters you feel are appropriate.

INTERVIEW CHEMISTRY: ONE SIMPLE RULE

Over the years there's been a lot of nonsense written on the topic of interview chemistry. Advice on maintaining eye contact, establishing personal rapport, emphasizing commonalities, and employing proper body language is fine in the abstract, but taken together, this advice has a tendency to make you forget what you're there for: to determine whether the possibility of a good fit exists between you and a potential employer.

Use common sense when thinking about whether to stare down your interviewer, squeeze the life out of his or her hand when you meet, claim overwhelming interest in everything the interviewer says and does, or maintain a single, stilted, supposedly "correct" posture during the interview. Rather than attempting to memorize a host of rules and guidelines in these areas, focus on *one* rule: Be yourself.

Relax. Show your true colors. Don't present yourself as desperate or as someone willing to say or do anything in order to get a job. Come across as *you.* Display confidence (not to be confused with arrogance), interest (not to be confused with fawning), and knowledge about the company's needs and objectives. Make it clear that you're interested in working for the company in question—that's both courtesy and sound strategy—but make it clear, too, that your self-image is not going to collapse if this opportunity doesn't come through for you.

Executives like to hire people who have a healthy, developed sense of who they are and what they want. Rather than trying to memorize a list of complicated instructions when it comes to fostering good chemistry between yourself and the interviewer, demonstrate the self-reliance and self-knowledge that will help you foster that positive chemistry effortlessly.

Don't pretend to be someone else. Let the employer get to know you as you really are: poised, confident, and under control.

"WHAT DO I SAY?"

Your aim in answering every interview question is to highlight four important working traits as second nature to you:

- You *take full responsibility* for everything that passes your desk and are comfortable prioritizing tasks as part of that job.
- You are willing to *go the extra mile,* including putting in extra hours when necessary.
- You are *flexible* and develop technical mastery of new systems easily.
- You are *organized and detail-oriented* and are adept at spotting errors large and small.

Rather than simply repeat these assertions for your interviewer's benefit, however, you will want to pass along anecdotes from your own working background that support them. The stories may overlap now and then, briefly incorporating one of the traits in question as a means of emphasizing another, but each story should, in the end, take one of the four characteristics above as its main theme.

Stories from real life are powerful. They dramatically highlight your strong suits, and they take one-on-one interview encounters out of the hypothetical realm and into the concrete. The stories also give your interviewer the chance to see you as a person with unique experiences and insights, rather than as another in a series of faceless applicants. Honing and developing a (truthful!) story from your own work life or earlier job search process—when combined with good personal chemistry—is probably the tactic most likely to win you a job offer. Spend some time on these stories. Think about the many and varied professional challenges you've faced over time. Take a little time in private to comb through your own background. Consider many possible incidents; write down their essentials on a notepad, and pick at least three, each of which strongly supports the four traits listed above.

What might these anecdotes might sound like? Here are some examples.

Assuming Full Responsibility. "Once, when my supervisor was on vacation, I was going over some instructions she'd left for me about delivering a new marketing plan to several executives at a firm that was considering granting our organization a contract. She'd also asked me to complete a training manual for an internal seminar that was to take place 3 or 4 months down the line. As I reviewed the marketing plan, which she and I had both assumed I would simply pop into an overnight package, I realized that it was incomplete—there was a whole section my supervisor apparently thought was complete that had been left out by a word processing secretary working on the project. The package was time-sensitive and represented several hundred thousand dollars in revenue, so I decided to put the training manual on hold and track down my manager's original notes. I went through everything, but I couldn't find the notes for the text she'd wanted to use; I couldn't track her down at her hotel, either. So I asked for a few moments of the vice president of marketing's time, explained what had happened, and asked if he could help me reconstruct the missing material. He was more than happy to do it. The result was that the marketing plan went out on time, and our company won the contract."

Going the Extra Mile. "My boss was on deadline once for a research project that was essential to our winning an important permit from the state government. As it happened, he came down with the flu at the worst possible time, and ended up doing a good deal of the work from home during the final week before the deadline. A few days before the project was due, though, he and I both realized that there was far more work remaining than he could complete on his own within the time we had. He faxed me a list of unresolved questions, and I headed over to the library to try to develop text material for the state. I was able to track down the material we needed by staying late at the library for the three nights in a row; I thought about driving over to his home and working side by side with him on the material, but I concluded, and my boss agreed, that one sick person on this project was one too many. After I overnighted all the new research to him, we put everything together by phone, him at his place and me at mine, in one last all-night session. The next morning, I passed everything over to one of my boss's colleagues for a final review, made a couple of corrections on the basis of her input, and drove the finished report over to the statehouse. We beat the deadline, and our organization received the permit we were after."

Ability to Adapt Flexibly to New Systems. "When we transferred over to a new system of tracking donors, my boss was a little nervous about things. This software had been custom-designed for us, and although we had plenty of technical support from the designers, we were planning a major fund-raising event, and we really didn't have much time to work. The initial version of any computer software is likely to have its share of problems, and this software was no exception. The first 2 days the system was up and running, I got in at 6:00 A.M.—and stayed until 7:00 P.M.—getting familiar with the new program, and running procedures similar to the ones we'd have to execute during the pledge drive that week. After checking every point in the manual and reviewing all my notes from my earlier meetings with the programmers, I was left with two fairly serious program bugs. I called the programmers as soon as I was sure of the extent of the problem, and they were able to develop fixes for both problems in time for me to start training people. The fund raiser went off without a hitch—we even exceeded our goal by 12 percent—and that system is still up and running today."

Detail Orientation. "I'm the type of person who believes in checking and double-checking things, even after they've been crossed off the list. Once, just to be on the safe side, my boss assigned me the task of reviewing all the copy for a new mail-order catalog we were completing, even though it had been reviewed by the people in the production department and was about to be sent to the printer. I was glad he did. There was an error on a tear-out subscription card and an internal pagination problem that everyone in production had missed! To be fair, both errors were the kinds that were easy to pass over: in very tiny type, the subscription card had a mistaken product code that referenced an entirely different piece of merchandise than the one cited, and the pagination problem was the result of confusing left- and right-hand pages. Each mistake, though, could have been extremely expensive if we hadn't caught it. The people in order fulfillment would have probably shipped the wrong product, and it's quite possible that the printer would have simply followed our instructions and printed the catalog incorrectly. Who knows how much time and money those problems would have cost the company! But that experience certainly made a believer out of me; it's safer to assume that there are errors waiting to be found than it is to assume that they've been caught. That's the operating principle I try to follow whenever I review something at work."

Notice how all the stories show an increased efficiency or more revenue for the company you worked for! Indicate exactly how your efforts benefited the employer, preferably in dollars and cents, organizational and procedural development, or time saved.

If you put your mind to it, you can come up with incidents from your own work or volunteer history that highlight each of these four key traits. Think about a time when things weren't going well on the job. (Certainly that isn't too difficult to do!) Weren't there a number of occasions when you had to step in and take the initiative to set things right? Jot down the details of several such stories; these are good starting points for your anecdotes concerning your ability to assume full responsibility for a positive outcome.

Think about a time when the place where you worked was dealing with a very challenging series of tasks that demanded the most from everyone. Wasn't there a situation in which you once had to or (preferably) volunteered to stay late, assumed extra duties, or pitchd in with an unorthodox solution? Commit the particulars of these incidents to paper; they will form the basis of the stories you use to highlight your willingness to go the extra mile. Be sure to incorporate the *positive outcome* of your efforts.

Think about a time when you had to make sense of a new system or organizational plan. These days computer systems change so quickly that virtually everyone can come up with a story along these lines without too much difficulty. What did you do to develop a working, pragmatic level of knowledge within the new system, enough to get the job done? Did you review a manual on your own initiative? Ask a supervisor for a few pointers? Wander through the system yourself to see what made sense? Commit all the relevant details to paper.

Think about an incident in which you were the bearer of bad news. For most of us, these are difficult events to forget! How many of these instances arose from errors or problems that you personally spotted? Write down all the details. Were you in charge of quality control, proofreading, or troubleshooting? What was the biggest, most important project you worked on? What kinds of errors did you flag? What would have happened had they gone unnoticed? Set all these facts down on paper as well. Your notes will help you develop anecdotes relating to your detail orientation.

Take the time *right now* to review your own personal background for the events outlined above. Spend at least 30 minutes developing the details of your various anecdotes. Write down as many facts as possible; you can select the most promising incidents later on in the process and rework the stories until you are in possession of a few shining jewels.

Do the work *now*—develop the essentials of your stories *now*—and you'll be glad you did when interview time rolls around!

ADVANCE PREPARATION

The beauty of preparing these stories in advance is that they can be adapted to any number of interview situations. You may have noticed how people in the public eye have a habit of tailoring prepared answers to tough questions, even though the questions, as posed, don't *exactly* match the answers offered. The idea is not to evade every question that comes your way (although we all know that any number of elected officials appear to do just that), but to stand your ground and display a sense of poise when a challenging question comes your way. You can do this by spontaneously adapting the closest possible matching response you've prepared. Fortunately, the four topics we've just covered—taking initiative, putting in extra effort, displaying flexibility, and maintaining an eye for detail—can be adapted to virtually any hypothetical problem that you must address.

Beware! Although you must prepare your story in advance, you must also take care not to sound as though you are tossing off a memorized speech word for word! Memorize the essentials of your anecdote, but do not attempt to recite a speech that sounds as though it's been forced, syllable by syllable, into your brain with a hammer.

If you don't have any work-related stories, then use your *personal* life experiences. What is important is to highlight your abilities in the aforementioned key areas.

Specific Questions You Should Anticipate

Some questions (e.g., "What's your greatest strength as a candidate?") practically scream to be united with one or more of the stories you've developed. Not *every* question posed during the interview will lend itself to the anecdotes you've prepared, however. Here's a list of common interview queries—and some detailed suggestions on how to respond to them.

- *Tell me a little bit about who you are and what you like to do.* This may also be phrased as "Tell me all about yourself." Even though the question, commonly used to begin an interview, sounds engaging and nonthreatening, it is actually a shrewd way of catching you off guard and gaining some insight into your priorities. Will you start talking about your favorite television shows, comic strips, or hobbies—or will you use this wide-open question to talk about the kinds of work contributions that make you feel most fulfilled?

- *What's your idea of the perfect job?* This one, of course. The more you know about the specific duties of the job for which you are applying, the better. (By the way, more than one job seeker has benefited during interview time from a decision to request a printed copy of the job description beforehand.) The messages you want to send here are fairly obvious: You enjoy balancing a number of responsibilities; you like working with other people; you relish a good challenge; you take pride in doing quality work; you are committed to lifetime learning.
- *Why are you qualified for this position?* Keep it short and sweet, and begin your answer with your strongest qualification. A long-winded answer to this one may do your candidacy more harm than good.
- *What do you see yourself doing 5 years from now?* Don't get too specific. You don't want to come across as someone with unrealistic expectations, or as the type of person who sets low goals. (You also want to put your interviewer at ease by letting him or her know that you're likely to stick around for a while.) Your best bet is to focus on your hope for ongoing growth within the position and your desire for personal satisfaction through making contributions that help the organization attain key goals. Make it clear that you feel that this position, this organization, and this industry match up well with your short- and long-term objectives.
- *Why are you interested in working here?* Your answer should reflect the research you have conducted into the target organization's operations. If you don't know *anything* about how this company operates, or what it does that matches your own interests, you should not expect to do well at the interview! Before the session you should, at the very least, request a copy of the company's annual report or a recent product/service brochure and study it closely in preparation for this question. Bear in mind that employers

are attracted to people who have a natural curiosity and a deep, abiding interest in company or division activities—people, in other words, who evidence a love of the work for its own sake. You certainly shouldn't mislead the prospective employer about the nature of your interest in the target organization's activities. By the same token, if you have followed this institution's product, service, or industry for some time and can cite evidence of a compelling personal fixation on the activities in question, it's definitely in your interest to do so when this question comes up! (And if this question *doesn't* come up, you shouldn't feel at all shy about highlighting your "research" when the opportunity presents itself. Enthusiasm of this kind can sometimes—not always, but sometimes—compensate for a résumé that does not boast all the formal requirements necessary for the position under consideration.)

- *Why do you want to leave your current employer?* Remember that badmouthing a current or former boss is not going to get you anywhere. Focus on your need for greater growth or challenge within the position rather than stating outright that you're "looking for more money." If you can, point to a logistical rather than personal hurdle—such as an unusually long commute or a desire to work closer to top decision makers—when outlining what is motivating you to seek employment elsewhere.
- *Why did you leave your previous employer?* Again, focus on logistical issues rather than the shortcomings of others. If you can supply evidence that you left your employer on good terms—a glowing endorsement, for instance—do so.
- *Do you think you're the type of person who works well under pressure?* Rather than answering yes and smiling pleasantly in anticipation of the next question, describe a time when you were able to deliver top-level results when the heat was on. It is worth noting here that executive assistants work under more or less constant pressure. If you can offer the interviewer solid proof of the fact that you know how to get not just any work, but your *best* work done during trying

times, this is the time to do so. If you have any doubts about your ability to work well under pressure, think twice about applying for this job.

- *What happened the last time someone criticized your work?* A sneaky one. The interviewer is trying to get you to either (1) supply an example of your own incompetence or (2) hold forth in detail on the various injustices visited upon you by a supervisor who didn't know as much as you did about something. Don't fall for either trap. Remember that the job for which you are applying is one in which you will have to focus, time and time again, on working out the kinks. What's more, you will *not* have the right to pound the table in the face of verbal criticism; instead, your job will be to roll with the punches and get all the feedback necessary to turn out superior work that makes your manager look great. Accordingly, you will need to hear this potentially difficult question as though it were phrased along the following lines: "Tell me about a time when you responded with perfect equanimity when someone criticized your work, used all the constructive criticism you could identify, saw past any indecorous or ill-conceived remarks, solved the problem at hand, and maintained good communication with the person who criticized you." Avoid the temptation to repeat any ill-chosen words your supervisor used in assessing your work, even if you plan to use them as an example of how you can maintain your composure when under attack. Focus on your ability to rectify areas that truly do need improvement; make it clear that you understand tense instructions are usually a fact of working life; demonstrate that you're not the kind who holds hastily chosen words against a manager.
- *What would you say if I told you I thought you were completely unqualified for this position?* Careful! Responding hastily with something equally rude—like "I'd say you were wrong" or "I'd probably conclude that I didn't really want this job after all"—would be a big mistake. This is what's known in the interviewing trade as a "stress question." Its sole purpose is to determine whether you are the type of candidate who's

likely to crumble under an assault. People applying for executive assistant positions are very likely to encounter such diabolical interview questions, because they do in fact have to weather the occasional attack from a manager. Before you go off the deep end in response to this question, or any of its deliberately abrasive variations, remember that prospective employers ask these imposing questions of only candidates they are very seriously considering hiring. So as rough as the question may sound on the surface, there's a very good chance that it signals a "buy" signal from the interviewer. (Admittedly, a stress question is not the most pleasant "buy" signal in the world to deal with, but trust me, it is in fact a positive sign.)

How, exactly, are you supposed to respond to a stress question? By showing the interviewer just what you're made of and making it clear that you're the type of worker who knows how to seek out important facts in a pressure-packed environment, tactfully and without returning fire. You might, for instance, respond to this question by informing the interviewer that, if this message were passed along to you, you'd ask for a written summary of the formal qualifications of the opening, to be passed along at the interviewer's convenience. You'd then review them closely and compare the requirements of the job to your own skill background. If you found that there were significant differences between the two, you'd report this—but you doubt this would be necessary, because, as you understand it, the position requires A, B, and C, which are, of course, three skills you possess in abundance.

Having quietly and calmly dealt with the facts and not the emotions inherent in the question as posed, you should sit back and await the next chance to demonstrate that you aren't the type to let an attack make you put your brain in neutral.

Warning. Stress questions can come at any time during the interview, and take the form of the most implausible questions or statements. Some of these verge on outright insult, but they must *not* be responded to as such. Stress probes could take the following unpleasant forms: *How could you say that? What makes you think something as silly as that? What do you mean, you've never done* X? (This is typically a forceful invitation for you to contradict yourself, one you should pleasantly decline, no matter what.) *How do you explain Y? What makes you think you'll make the grade here? What would you say if I told you I'd already decided to give this job to someone else?* (This may be reserved for you as you walk out the door of what seems to have been a superb interview performance!) In all cases, your aim is to keep your cool, show that you know how to deal with difficult situations, and keep from polarizing the situation.

- *What do you do for fun?* Even though this may *seem* like the perfect opportunity to provide details about your favorite television program, you're better off citing some (1) group or (2) solo activity that supports your candidacy. If you choose to mention a group activity, outline one that illustrates your ability to deal well with others in a social setting, and make it clear that this mirrors your team mentality when it comes to workplace relationships. If you choose to discuss a solo undertaking, your best bet is probably to mention a recent book you've read that illustrates both your mindset and your ability to draw important work-related lessons from outside sources. Stay away from controversial hobbies and topics. Whatever you do, prepare *something* in response to this question; it is among the most common of all interview queries, and answering it with a long pause or a desperate bit of improvisation won't do much to aid your cause.

  This is a demanding job. How did you decide that this was the work you wanted to do? Describe the decision-making process that led you to commit to this line of work. The more systematized and logical the process is, the better off your candidacy will be. (Obviously, an answer that leaves the impression that you undertake serious decisions of this kind on a whim won't do your cause much good.) If you can, detail the research that went into the selection of this employer, and highlight the areas of strongest fit between your work background and the culture and objectives of the organization.

OF TESTS AND TEST TAKING

It's quite possible that your interview will include clerical and other proficiency tests. In Appendix III of this book, you will find some samples of tests we at The Duncan group administer to new candidates.

TIME TO GO

Near the conclusion of your interview, you'll be asked something along the lines of, "Do you have any questions for me before we wrap up?" Don't answer in the negative; ask *one or two* intelligent questions. (Don't ask about salary or benefits at this point; don't pepper the interviewer with rapid-fire queries.) Here are some of the questions you should consider posing as the interview heads for the finish line:

How did you get started at this company?

What do you think is the biggest challenge this company faces right now?

How would you describe this company's mission?

Broadly speaking, what kind of role do you envision for this person?

What's the main thing you're hoping this person will be able to get accomplished?

What do you think the typical day would look like?

What do you think is the most important skill required for someone to fulfill this job?

Let the person you're talking to answer the questions you've posed at length. Then smile, shake hands, thank your contact for his or her time, and say something along the following lines:

> Ms. Smith, I want you to know that I think this position sounds very exciting, and I hope you're considering me as seriously as I'm considering you. My feeling is that this company and I represent an excellent potential match, and I think I could make an important contribution here.

> Before I go, I want you to know that this position is exactly what I'm looking for. I hope you'll decide to give me the chance to work with you, and I promise you that you won't regret doing so.

As it turns out, that last sentence, or some variation on it, may be the most important part of your entire interview. Why? Well, remember that one of the most important things people look for in an executive assistant, and in many of the positions that lead up to that job, is *accountability.* As you've no doubt gathered, one of the chief distinguishing characteristics of the new executive assistant is the ability, even the eagerness, to assume full responsibility for something that's challenging or fraught with technical uncertainties. Assuming you can back it up, that promise to succeed in a demanding job is a clear signal to the person considering hiring you that you don't shy away from making commitments. You enjoy doing so. That's a great message to pass along as the interview draws to a close.

Take full responsibility!

FOLLOWING UP

During your interview you've made a point of demonstrating your poise, tact, persistence, and ability to stay on top of things. Your follow-up campaign, which you should pursue *whether or not you receive the job offer,* should display all the same elements.

If you do not yet know whether you will be offered the position, you should follow up by writing a personal one-page note to your interviewer. Unless your handwriting is impeccable, this letter should be word-processed. It should be mailed no later than the day after your interview. You should thank your contact for his or her time, and restate your desire to work for the company.

If you receive word later that you have not been offered the position, don't write this prospective employer off! Staying in contact with the people who have interviewed you is one of the most important steps of your job search. Write *another* one-page letter, on a positive note. Mention that you thoroughly enjoyed the chance to discuss employment opportunities at the company in question, and ask that your contact keep you in mind in the event any other opportunities arise.

"THEY'VE OFFERED ME THE JOB!"

That's wonderful!

If you haven't given the employer an unwavering pledge to report for work, and if you still don't know as much as you might like about the company that's offering you a job, it's time to take stock of the situation. Before you say "count me in"...

Take a good, long look at the company where you would be working. Does it match your working style? If you are gregarious and eager to interact with people—certainly good traits for someone who hopes to become an executive assistant—are you hooking up with a supervisor or an employer who feels that your role should be more reminiscent of "sit here and do the work and don't talk to anyone"?

Do you have a good rapport with the person for whom you'll be working? This is not the same as having a similar *personality* to that of your supervisor; in fact, pleasantly contrasting personalities, of the kind that allow the two of you to cover all aspects of a vexing problem between you, are probably better predictors of success in this job. Your aim is to land a job in which you feel comfortable interacting with your manager on a day-to-day basis. Beware of managers who seem to have everything in common with you—and by the same token, of those who seem unlikely to invest *any* time or energy into the development of a good working relationship, other than to bark orders from time to time.

Is the salary commensurate with your skills and experience? To answer this question, you may want to research the salaries of positions comparable to the one you've just been offered, or ask those in your own personal contact network about the competitiveness of the offer that's been extended. Don't forget to include the value of health insurance or other perks.

CHAPTER THREE

THE INFORMATION REVOLUTION—AND WHY PEOPLE, NOT TECHNOLOGY, COME FIRST

The open society, the unrestricted access to knowledge, the unplanned and uninhibited association of men for its furtherance—these are what may make a vast, complex, ever-growing, ever-changing, ever more specialized and expert technological world, nevertheless a world of human community.

—J. Robert Oppenheimer

The driving force in business today has to be the revolutionary new ways our organizations are finding to manage massive amounts of information. We've developed so many means of harnessing the latest technological advances, and we keep replacing them at such a breathtaking pace, that it's hard not to conclude that these advances represent the single most important factor in our daily work routine.

How will the current technological revolution shape our future? To answer that, let's think for just a moment about how the technology of the past has *usually* redefined the world of work.

Each dramatic technological advance in our history has heralded significant social change and helped the societies they affected move on to new levels of intelligence, achievement, and creativity. Not all the change has been painless. Not all the advantages have come overnight. But these two factors, social change and enhanced achievement, have been closely linked during times of great technological development. Early in the century, for instance, the automobile made the horse and buggy obsolete—but created millions of new jobs.

Sometimes technological changes don't wipe out entire business sectors but do radically transform the world in which businesses must operate. During the 1930s and 1940s, Americans were truly movie house addicts; millions of men, women, and children visited the local cinema on a weekly, or sometimes even daily, basis. With the advent of television, however, the national love affair with the local picture house was suddenly over, and movie executives had to find new ways to attract audiences. Although the film industry survived, its ornate, single-screen palaces, once attended with nearly religious fervor by countless movie fans, did not. Because they could turn on instant entertainment at home any time they felt like it, people simply stopped going to the movies as much as they had in the past.

The horse and buggy may have been a more pleasant and leisurely means of getting from one place to another than a modern compact car; the gilded proscenium of the local cinema may have been a more idyllic setting for movie fans than today's suburban multiplex; yet people opted in huge numbers for newer ways of doing things, buggies are now for romantic evening drives around the park, and profitable single-screen movie theaters are rare businesses indeed.

Today, the information revolution brings us to a similar threshold. A new generation of incredibly sophisticated technologies is being introduced into our work stations. For some, the new ways of doing things will be profoundly threatening. For others, the very unpredictability of the period we live in—its constant innovation, its propensity for unleashing new and more powerful software and computers only months after we've mastered the old systems—will herald a time of unparalleled opportunity and growth.

The sharp drop in the cost of computing power has changed forever the old notion of what a support person does. More and more often, it's the technology that's doing the supporting, rather than the people. Customer service representatives at

NYNEX, the regional phone company, for instance, have gone from being conduits for information about a few selected products to problem-resolving experts on virtually all customer requests. Powerful new software allows them to answer billing questions, schedule new installations, and perform any number of other tasks that were once the province of several different departments whose efforts had to be carefully coordinated. The new system, which guides human operators through a seemingly infinite sea of responses to consumer questions, is so well designed—and covers so much ground—that relatively little training and updating is required to operate it.

Computer-aided laser technology has helped Ford Motor Company reduce its prototype part development cycle by as much as 30 weeks. That's 30 fewer weeks of memos going back and forth; 30 fewer weeks of phone messages to take down; 30 fewer weekly meetings to attend and chronicle.

Computers now have the ability to make logical inferences and to process information in essentially the same way our brains do. These computers can gather information on hundreds, even thousands of different variables at a time, and can prepare accurate forecasts on a wide variety of subjects: the likelihood of a motion picture's becoming a box office hit, say, or even what the weather will be like a month from now! Other computers are capable of taking sophisticated verbal dictation and can make distinctions among 20,000 spoken words!

In years past, the sight of a motorized piece of machinery was something remarkable, an impossible-to-ignore symbol of technological progress. Now such technology is hardly noticed at all; motors are built into our lives in thousands of ways, from automobiles to food processors, from elevators to refrigerators, from wheelchairs to home heating units. In the post-World War II period, motors became so commonplace that they were very nearly invisible.

We now live in a world in which computers are steadily becoming invisible in much the same way. We may not think that we're operating computers when we check our home phone machine for messages during a business trip, or make a withdrawal from a bank machine, or send someone a birthday card that plays a tune when it's opened, but that's just what we're doing. And the pace of the expansion of computer technology is accelerating at what must be considered, in historical terms at least, nearly incalculable speed. The birthday card that plays a tune contains in its circuitry more computing power than existed on the entire face of the earth before the year 1950.

Microchip capacity—that is to say, the basic computing ability offered in the most advanced chips—doubles every 18 months. In his recent book *The Physics of Immortality,* mathematical physicist Frank Tipler estimates that the amount of time it will now take for science to develop a computer capable of holding an on-screen conversation indistinguishable from human discourse is about 30 years. Just to put it in perspective, that means we are further away in time from the Beatles's first appearance on *The Ed Sullivan Show* than we are from being able to strike up an informal conversation with a computer about the local baseball team, or for that matter, the likelihood of life after death.

The dizzying pace of today's technological breakthroughs is probably unprecedented in human history. Every day, it seems, we find ourselves introduced to new and dramatic innovations, some of them so advanced that they challenge our ability to comprehend them. And yet…

And yet the current emphasis in the business world is on people.

Team-centered achievement. Team-oriented goals. Team-first work groups. Teams that use new technology to take on the work that used to be done by two, three, or more departments. It would be a mistake, certainly, to ignore the dramatic role that downsizing has played in reshaping the landscape of the American workforce. But it would also be a mistake to ignore the new, more challenging demands made of those critical, technologically adept workers who find themselves important players in today's reconstituted, reconfigured companies—or in fast-moving entrepreneurial outfits that didn't undergo downsizing in the first place.

These new-era knowledge workers are not focusing on carrying out orders, keeping their ideas to themselves, and toeing the corporate line. They are gathering together in loosely organized work groups—remarkably powerful ones, by the standards of anyone familiar with the hierarchical organizations of some years back. These workers are using technology to develop newer and more effective ways of carrying out the organization's mission, and, not infrequently, they are showing up at work in the morning to find that their suggestions and feedback are actually being implemented.

Many of today's information analysts find that they are at the heart of things in a way they never were at earlier phases of their careers, and perhaps never expected to be. What they say, think, and report about customers, service, processes, procedures, and operations suddenly *matters,* largely because of advanced communications technology. And, very often, there are fewer layers of bureaucracy for them to wade through in order to get across important pieces of information to customers or management. When you have the president of the company's e-mail address, and when she regularly writes back, it's hard to spend too much time complaining about how little access you have to the top echelons of the organization.

Today's workers may find themselves staring at tight schedules, but they also have the opportunity to use technology to make contacts with people at all levels, to become freer, to do more, to learn more, and to gain greater insight into the global economy. It's a busy time, but it's also incredibly exhilarating.

THE NEW OUTLOOK

This is the state of affairs at many—not all, admittedly, but many—of the most successful companies in our technology-driven economy. Be aware that the new working principle of many of our most dynamic corporations, a principle fueled in large measure by technological advances, assumes that increases in productivity are the result of new, more communicative models for the very idea of work. These models focus on much less restrictive job descriptions than most of us ever imagined possible, team-oriented work groups, formal employee input when dealing with issues that require problem solving, and higher degrees of employee involvement in all areas of the business.

All of this means: Quicker feedback from the front lines, where the customer makes his or her decisions. A nimble set of management philosophies that at least attempts to set group cohesiveness and simplicity of structure as important business goals, and not infrequently, carries through on those attempts. The long overdue encouragement of senior managers to *listen* to what employees have to say about the things that matter most: product and service quality, effective practices, and organizational savvy.

These are the hallmarks of the ongoing information explosion. I think you'll agree that this is a very exciting time indeed to be alive, a very exciting time to be working on the cutting edge. Because at long last people have emerged as the most important elements of any venture. And the long-delayed ascendancy of the human being can be traced, paradoxically enough, to the ascendancy of human technology. People are essential—because only people can make intelligent decisions on the basis of gargantuan amounts of new information that are a fact of business life nowadays.

No one is saying that upheavals and changes in the working world have not occurred over the past 10 to 15 years. But the net result has been, time and time again, the consolidation of staggering amounts of information. Those who know how to access and act intelligently on that information *matter* to their employers, and far more than anyone could have imagined just a few short years ago.

Yes, you read right. In the new era of information, *people matter.* We matter!

If.

Yes, there is a catch.

We matter…if. *If* we commit to adapting to technology as it unfolds; and as we have seen, it is unfolding at a nearly incalculable rate. *If* we make an effort to understand new business practices. *If* we learn how global practices influence advancement. *If* we don't fall into the trap of avoiding the newest, most unfamiliar ways of managing information. *If* we cultivate adaptability as a career survival skill (of which more is to be said in the next chapter). Those are big ifs.

TOSSING ASIDE OLD ASSUMPTIONS

For those who hesitate to take advantage of the new ways of doing things—those who fail to update their skills and develop new ones as the need arises—the going will be rough. But we don't have to make those mistakes. Not if we look clearly at our situation.

In today's complex, constantly shifting economy, the number of clear rules for company strategists to follow as they chart their organization's course is often vexingly few. It bears repeating: Today's top decision makers aren't looking for people who will simply carry out instructions. They're looking for people who can be counted on to add value, to supply key insights, breakthroughs, and updates, and to use technology in a pragmatic way to help keep margins (often razor-thin ones) intact. Such duties often break or rewrite as many rules as they initiate.

This is not to say that insubordination and seat-of-the-pants guesswork are the cornerstones of contemporary career success. But it's worth remembering that employers are, more and more, on the lookout for trustworthy, open-minded employees who don't need rigid hierarchies and clearly defined structures in order to be efficient and productive.

TAKING CONTROL—WITHOUT TAKING OVER

As you may have gathered, professional careers in general, and a career as an executive assistant in particular, now place a greater emphasis than ever before on personal initiative and observation. Whether it takes the form of sighting the latest technological curveball to hurtle your way, assuming responsibility for your own training and development, or rethinking the implications of a long-standing company policy and making a creative suggestion as a result, your work will—must—be marked by more independent thought and action than your predecessors, if only because today's technology will enable you to *do* something, or *learn* something, more quickly than your predecessors.

As an effective executive assistant, you will work to support your manager in the midst of an array of challenges that you know you will not be able to identify. You will also be in possession of more knowledge about key events than the vast majority of your coworkers. That means you'll face some of the greatest challenges, as well as some of the greatest opportunities. You'll need to keep your balance, keep your manager informed, keep a step ahead of the latest crisis, *and* keep up with the latest technological developments affecting your industry.

That's a pretty heavy workload. How are you going to handle it all? In the next chapter we'll look in detail at the major challenges executive assistants are likely to face in the years to come—and at some of the best strategies for managing the inevitable changes, both technological and organizational, both domestic and global, that may come your way.

CHAPTER FOUR

IN PRAISE OF ADAPTABILITY

Don't fight forces; use them.

—R. Buckminster Fuller

Meet Alice in Deadline-land.

The boss regarded Alice with a distinctly disapproving gaze. "Am I to understand," he said warily, "that you plan to go *home*? Despite the work still to be done on finding out about that new market we're chasing?"

"Why yes, sir," Alice responded quietly. "It's nearly eight in the evening, and I've been here since dawn."

"Alice, Alice, Alice," said the boss, shaking his head slowly, "this is no longer the me decade of the 1980s, but the *commitment* decade of the 1990s. You simply *must* put in more hours. I fully expect you to put in at least, oh, 200 hours every week."

"Well, one can't work that many hours," Alice objected. "There *aren't* that many hours in a week. Even if you worked round the clock and never slept, you could never work more than 168 hours in a single week."

"You could if your family chipped in," the boss shouted triumphantly.

CHANGE IS UNAVOIDABLE—AND IT HAS A WAY OF FILLING UP YOUR SCHEDULE

I think anyone who's had to master the details of a completely new product line in weeks, rather than months, would agree that rapid change has a way of bulldozing through a neatly arranged list of to-do items. So would anyone who's watched an entire budget year's worth of computer equipment go from a state-of-the-art system to a fossilized tax write-off in what seems like a matter of minutes. Change, and specifically technological change, can be pretty daunting sometimes. It can make a day that you thought was as full as it could possibly get…get even fuller. And that certainly keeps things interesting around the office.

Even if we're not always enthusiastic about trying to make forward progress in today's challenging business environment, most of us don't really have the option of simply throwing up our hands and saying "No thank you!" when faced with the prospect of rapid change. Those of us who must help the key people in our organizations make informed decisions, turn on a dime when market conditions demand it, and meet ever more intense competitive challenges to retain our customer base—those of us, in other words, who occupy the positions traditionally identified as executive assistants—must somehow find a way to meet the demands we face. The good news is that we *can* do so—if we and the organizations we work for are willing to look at things in new ways. The bad news, as we've seen, is that if we decide that things *look* impossible from a traditional frame of reference and are not "part of what we do," we're in trouble.

The new realities of the economy we face as the twenty-first century dawns are sobering. Individuals and organizations that do not learn to accommodate themselves to the constantly changing business conditions around them may suddenly occupy the same position in which George Burns found himself when he realized he might be getting old after all. Burns recalled once that he awoke one morning only to discover that just about everything hurt, and that whatever *didn't* hurt didn't do what it was supposed to anymore.

In other words, organizations that fail to learn how to make change and adaptability a key skill at all levels can expect to get very old, very fast. By the same token, those organizations that do learn that lesson will stay young—and win the competitive battles ahead. Executive assistants are among the most important players in fostering adaptability to change, even change that may seem impossible at first. In doing so we will help our organizations, and our own careers. But we will have to do so by mastering a variety of new roles, ones we may not have anticipated. And we will have to dispel a number of long-held myths.

THREE MYTHS

There are three myths we must dispense with when considering the challenges the executive assistant is likely to face in the twenty-first century. The first of these, and perhaps the most important to dispel, is the idea that we can expect to find a good job whose duties will remain essentially unchanged for any significant stretch of time.

Companies are finding more efficient ways to satisfy their customers and clients. They will continue to find more efficient ways to satisfy their client base for the rest of our working lives, and we should get used to that. The continuing explosion in information technology will allow companies to operate with less and less tolerance for inefficiency. What is standard operating procedure today probably won't be tomorrow.

What's more, in the new economy anything that vaguely resembles what we once called "clerical work" is simply not worth establishing as the foundation of your career. A good percentage of the hundreds of thousands of jobs that have been eliminated over the past 5 years or so went on the chopping block because companies found more effective ways to manage information than they had previously.

The second myth to get rid of is the one suggesting that what's in the warehouse is what matters most. We must acquaint ourselves with the idea that in most business settings intellectual capital is the most critical company resource in attracting and retaining customers. Not inventory. Not machinery. Not bushels of wheat. Not chunks of metal. But the intangible assets of skill, knowledge, and information, resulting in that ultimate company resource: ideas. Ideas on how to implement our own changes, ideas on how to react to the changes of our competitors, ideas, ultimately, on how to attract and retain customers. Where then, does this leave Alice—the executive assistant? Provided she is willing to offer innovation when it comes to working with, and making the most of, the organization's intellectual capital, she will find she is in a more promising position than almost anyone else in the organization.

That's because the third myth has to do with organization; it's the idea that Alice is, by virtue of the nature of her job, far removed from the new tools and new opportunities she needs to make things happen (and, with any luck, get home before midnight). The most exciting new feature of the revolution in information technology has to do with the changing nature of our work groups. In the new economy many layers of authority are a distinct *disadvantage* in accommodating wave upon wave of new information. Relatively autonomous team-oriented work groups are better suited to the fast-paced world in which we live and work. The new technologies have given many customer-focused companies, particularly those in the service sector, the ability to react quickly to competitive pressures and to grow at truly staggering speeds.

As we have seen, computing power, even though it changes hardware and software incarnations rapidly, is more affordable than many had ever dreamed it would be. It has allowed the most dynamic organizations to free up their employees so they can focus on fulfilling their commitments to the customer as never before. Those organizations that are prepared to implement the new technologies, and put their people's energies toward the task of maintaining a competitive edge, rather than shuffling papers or managing cumbersome hierarchies, will find that the potential for market success is truly remarkable. And those who help *implement* the new technologies (read: Alice) are in an excellent position to reap more significant career benefits than ever.

That's three changes, and for most of us, they're big ones:

- Job descriptions are more or less meaningless in the long run.
- Ideas and information count more than just about anything else at the organization's disposal.
- The hierarchical structure most of us grew up associating with the world of business is no longer a working model.

Those of us who already hold positions in organizations that are struggling to manage or initiate internal change may sometimes feel confused or uncertain when we see evidence of these unparalleled alterations in our economy. But behind the seemingly endless news stories about layoffs lies a new wave of exciting opportunity. This opportunity is reserved, however, for those who are committed to helping the organization make the most of its resources and deliver on its aims. And that is something we cannot expect to do by identifying a few specific tasks and simply repeating them. The skill we must master is adaptability itself.

THE CHALLENGES OF THE FUTURE

So much for the broad outline of the horizon. What are the specific challenges facing the executive assistant likely to be in the years to come? There are a number of areas to keep an eye on, and I want to review them now.

I'd like to preface the following observations by emphasizing that what underlies any progress in any position in the new economy is the commitment to focus on the customer, whether that's the one inside the company who gets your work directly, or the one at the end of the line who uses the product or service. Please remember that the business world we live in today demands that we assume responsibility and accountability for our work, rather than for the formal requirements of any job title—even the requirements I'm outlining here.

In today's team-first environment the point is not to be distracted by titles and status, but to focus on your ability to deliver exemplary results and roll with the inevitable changes that will come your way.

THE EXECUTIVE ASSISTANT MUST HELP THE ORGANIZATION EASE THE TRANSITION TO THE WORKPLACE OF THE FUTURE

The physical configuration of the workplace of the future is likely to be far different from the segmented, departmentalized structures most of us know. The executive assistant can play a key role in helping her organization make the transition to new, and initially unfamiliar, office layouts.

In their book *Workplace by Design*, Franklin Becker and Fritz Steele offer an open, team-oriented office floor plan. Their ideas suggest that by minimizing barriers between groups, we will help our organizations incorporate the fast-moving, ever-changing patterns of work they will have to embrace if we hope to succeed in the business environment of the years to come. Becker and Steele compare standard, old-style organizational floor plans to relay races in which a single initiative emerges from a high-level conference room and makes its way in a straight line through predetermined points in the organization. They argue that the more efficient model for today's team-oriented workforces is the amoebalike movement of a rugby team, in which key players can change with almost dizzying speed. With this rugby-team model in mind, Becker and Steele suggest an open workplace with distinct "activity zones" that encourage employees to work wherever they are most effective as their day progresses. There are fewer barriers, physical and otherwise, in such a workplace. In many such settings, food and drink are available throughout the day, employees schedule their own breaks, and teams get greater exposure to one another than would be the case if they were working in cubicles or behind closed doors. Such an environment, Becker and Steele argue, increases efficiency, reduces the amount of friction or enmity between work groups, and puts much-needed emphasis on the ability to perform a number of different tasks in a variety of environments.

That's one intriguing idea that may influence the physical layout of the office of the future. Now what tools do we expect that office to contain? I believe the executive assistant will be one of the most important players in the organization when it comes to helping it make new technologies land in the right spot and do what they're supposed to. Accordingly, it seems worthwhile now to review some of the changes in office technology that we're all likely to face in the very near future.

Although the computer and software industries are erratic ones in which consensus about emerging trends is hard to come by (and predictions often turn out to be surrealistically off-base), some respected figures have gone out on a limb and taken some guesses at what the future will hold for the modern office. Paradoxically, one of the few things on which most experts *do* agree is that, for much of the time, it won't be an office at all. Thanks to increasingly effective communications technology, a major trend will continue: making off-site time productive time, both for homeworkers and for executives whose duties take them to remote locations, will continue. That means that the human being left in the middle—and, at top levels, that means the executive assistant—will play a more critical role than ever in making sure all the proper bases get touched. Anyone who's tried to get a new piece of equipment up and running for the first time while on the road knows how important that function is.

In addition to making the most efficient use of our time outside the office, it's quite possible that, once we walk in the door again, we'll be dealing with office computers that don't *look* much like computers at all. Executives at Acer America are talking about desks with flat built-in display pads and personal filing cabinet devices the size of bricks. Other firms, such as Displaytech, are predicting computers that will be roughly the size of cigarette packs that come with a high-resolution display the size of sunglasses. (Displaytech has perfected a full-color working prototype of such a portable display.)

And these new machines will be connected as never before. At AT&T, for instance, new and emerging software such as automated workflow programs will allow individual pieces of information management equipment to blur traditional distinctions between, say, a computer and a telephone. The software people are now talking about products that will act on behalf of absent workers, using logical constructs to sort and route incoming electronic communications.

As if that weren't mind-boggling enough, Montreal's QMS Canada was recently touting a product called the QMS 2001 Knowledge System that incorporates a self-contained PC and can also be configured to run on an external system. The machine manages both paper and electronic messages, and its manufacturers claim that before too long, it will also integrate voice, telephone, audio, video, and network connectivity. It will, they say, be able to coordinate a videoconference, send a one-way video message, and even remotely read faxes to a user by telephone.

Separately, these changes leave one reeling. Taken together, however, they point to something very important about the environments in which we will soon work. More fundamental than any one of the possible advances I've mentioned is the new way our organizations are going to start thinking of data in the first place. The office of the not-too-distant future is going to find ways to make more harmonious use of information than ever before. It is going to make its various applications amazingly compatible, and it will start processing information in a totally new way. As Hewlett-Packard VP and General Manager Richard Watts puts it in a recent interview, the office equipment of tomorrow is not going to be a collection of disparate machines, but rather components of a single, massive information utility. Quoting Watts now, "We think one day checking into a hotel room and not finding an information appliance, like a PC will be a surprise. An information appliance must be something that is seamless and available without you having to think about it. It would provide a way to access, manipulate, and retransmit information."

Does this mean we will soon use an office in which no one needs help getting what he or she wants? To the contrary. Watts offers a surprisingly frank assessment of the ongoing challenges inherent in any massive information system. He says, "Not only are the utilities and tools that we've got today not really designed for this massively distributed network, but it's also a function of the very complexity of what you're trying to deal with. I mean, there is not going to be a simple way to access every piece of information in the world."

The picture some years hence, then, is of an office that is more streamlined and perhaps less task-oriented than the one we now use. Accessing new information, however, and incorporating the ever-more-ingenious tools designed for accessing it are going to remain significant organizational challenges *for the rest of our lives*. It is because of these changes that I believe the executive assistant who follows a generalist career path (about which more later) will be in a perfect position to help the organization deal with those challenges.

This transition-easing role, combined with some key organizational functions, is a part of the job that the executive assistant *must* embrace without losing sight of her existing responsibilities.

The Executive Assistant Must Simultaneously Embrace Old and New Job Functions

Technology will continue to change the work environment; the pervasiveness of such changes will increase the need for continuous flexibility.

Today's executive is more likely to type in his or her own correspondence, send his or her own e-mail, and manage his or her own message traffic than before. There is a large and steadily rising generation of executives who will relinquish their laptop computer only when someone pries it from their cold, dead fingers—or when a model that allows them to get more accomplished becomes available.

Executive assistants must be willing to help implement all the new systems and keep the old ones up and running for those who won't part from them. They must be willing to embrace anything and everything that helps their organizations win and retain its customers, and they must keep their managers' schedules straight while they do this!

In brief, they must make sense of the new without abandoning the old.

Maintaining poise in the face of a sudden work overload or an unexpected shift of responsibilities isn't exactly fun, but it is possible to achieve. There are three important areas of development that can help you make a little more sense of the changing technological workplace. If you make an ongoing personal commitment to improve in these areas, my guess is that you will find the process of accommodating yourself to new workplace situations somewhat easier.

- *Be willing to make judgment calls when it comes to managing your own time—and be willing to stand behind them.* As we have seen, the successful organization is willing to put more responsibility into the hands of workers for whom decision making has not, historically, been a high priority. (You'll remember that the ability to make steadily more difficult decisions, and to be held accountable for them, is part of the career path that leads toward the executive assistant role. Once you're in the job, decisions affecting your ability to manage your own time effectively are likely to be among the most important of all!)

  That power to make choices extends to your own ability to schedule and to determine and execute priority decisions, so you should not be afraid to instill procedures and practices that work for you when it comes to managing your workload. You should, however, be willing to justify all the decisions you make in terms of a mutually accepted objective.
- *Attain more product knowledge.* One consequence of the breathtakingly rapid exchange of information is that cus-

tomers have become smarter and pickier. They have broad exposure to many more products and services than they had in the past, and on the whole they are becoming more discriminating about those products and services they buy. In many markets, they have even found that they are relieved of geographical boundaries when they make purchases. It's estimated that the national 800-number system generates 22 *billion*—that's billion, with a *b*—calls every year. Televised consumer outlets have been a market force to be reckoned with for several years; Internet- and cable-box-based consumer technologies are not far behind.

If the new economic landscape sends any message, it is that the customer is in charge as never before, and that the competition to build a customer relationship is going to be stiff. (And, by the way, new information technologies help to make *internal* customers pickier, too!)

It follows that everyone in the organization, but particularly the executive assistant, must be familiar with exactly what the organization has to offer that impatient, demanding prospective customer. The days when so-called administrative staff could avoid bothering themselves with the details of who buys the company's product, and why, are long over. In organizing your day, base your decisions as much as possible on how a given task will advance a customer-related concern or improve the organization's product or service. This is a standard that you and your manager can both buy into.

- *Use the knowledge you have to build new alliances.* During reorganization and reengineering, the executive assistant may be one of the most important team members when it comes to helping confused or threatened employees come to terms with their new roles. She may also be able to fend off certain technical problems before they arise. In environments that shortchange training and support, she may be one of the few reliable sources of important information about data systems, and that means she'll be in an excellent position to reinforce larger organizational goals for her manager. (In the manager's absence, she may also be the only person in the organization who knows which members of different groups should be talking to one another!)

Developing new interteam contacts and smoothing the way for others during these times of transformation are good ways to build alliances. And alliances are what help keep things from falling apart.

THE EXECUTIVE ASSISTANT MUST BE BOTH GENERALIST AND *INTRAPRENEUR*

As I've noted earlier, learning to look beyond formal labels and job descriptions is a critical part of success in the new economy. One of the biggest transitions we have to make is a change in the very nature of the word *employee,* which once seemed to be an unshakable concept. Fortunately, the two new connotations attached to the once straightforward *employee* are not really difficult to grasp.

In the new economy we must be pretty good at a lot of different things, rather than really good at just one or two; and on occasion we must be willing to think like an entrepreneur.

For the executive assistant, whose job can be compared to that of an octopus on roller skates, an air traffic controller on a foggy night, or even a combination trapeze artist and Zen master, the transition toward both generalist and intrapreneur roles may be easier than it is for others in the organization. After all, this person must be familiar with time zones, geography, which hotels are close to what airports, techniques for dealing with different global communications systems, strategic planning, accounting, phone etiquette, and office skills, and, last but not least, must have the ability to look calm when things are exploding. So I believe an effective executive assistant is up for the challenges that face her in the coming years. Unforeseen developments are her stock-in-trade!

You must commit to being a generalist. Others may choose to find a tiny corner of the technology to master inside and out in the hope that they, and only they, will be able to respond to each and every query that may arise. But the working world in which we now live usually makes more pragmatic demands. The new environment forces us to accept the fact that we don't, and probably shouldn't, have all the answers. It asks not that we master every inch of a new procedure, but that *we develop the skills necessary to master enough of it to get the job done,* and that we be ready to do the same in short order with the *next* system, which won't be long in coming.

In his book, *The Third Wave,* Alvin Toffler notes that future employers will need people who accept responsibility, who understand how their work dovetails with that of others, who can handle even larger tasks, who adapt swiftly to changed circumstances, and who are sensitively tuned in to the people around them.

In the years to come, workers in general—and executive assistants in particular—will be increasingly rewarded for their ability to develop the skills of generalists rather than for their deep knowledge in a specific field. As an executive coordinator, you must often act as the eyes and ears of a senior executive, and that means you will need to make sense of many different types of information. Your challenge will be to develop professionally as technology illuminates new models for your organization. You will have to be close to day-to-day business issues and aware of new strategic developments. In many cases you will need to act as a sounding board and provide feedback before a policy or new initiative is finalized. Often, you will learn by doing—and you will be among the first in the organization to do so.

That may seem like plenty to deal with, but as we've seen, today's economic conditions demand that we add a measure of the entrepreneur to the mix as well. For many of us, that's an unfamiliar role. If I had to identify a single attribute of the entrepreneur that executive assistants would do well to emulate, it would have to be the ability to see and adapt to new possibilities. After all, when we see and adapt to new possibilities, we initiate a little change of our own, and we do so on our own terms.

Being an intrapreneur does not mean overstepping boundaries; it means:

- Working with top management to cut across old boundaries
- Making the commitment to challenge your own abilities
- Getting the information you need
- Accepting a goal that makes sense for the organization
- Working harmoniously with others to make decisions, establishing appropriate benchmarks, and taking responsibility for what happens as a result of your efforts

Executive assistants have a twin allegiance: to their managers, and to the unending aim of helping the organization find and satisfy the customer. In today's flattened, customer-sensitive workplaces, that's not a contradiction at all. It's a challenge to the entrepreneurial spirit.

That spirit sometimes takes the form of suggesting revisions in company policy. Indeed, simplification of fat books full of rules and regulations is one of the hallmarks of successful reengineering. Employees who aren't handcuffed by incomprehensible regulations do a better job of keeping customers satisfied, but de-handcuffing them may take a little work. The executive assistant can be one of the most important players in the essential job of condensing the volumes of guidelines into a few critical principles.

The executive assistant is also in a perfect position to use entrepreneurial thinking to make the most of the organization's most important capital—information. Who in the organization is better suited to help make that data accessible to team members at all levels than the adaptive, broadly skilled executive assistant?

The Executive Assistant Must Help Institute Important Structural Changes

For many of us, adapting to the economic changes of the past few years has been a little like waking up in a strange new land. That can be a disorienting experience at first, but it can also be profoundly exciting when one realizes the new possibilities of the unexplored surroundings.

As we have seen, the distance between executive and administrative work is getting shorter all the time. Free-floating teams, loosely structured and arranged so as to emphasize creativity and sensitivity to the most recent customer concerns, are the order of the day. The executive assistant must be ready to make contributions to such teams and to report important developments to her manager. In so doing, she fulfills one of the most important functions in the entire organization.

Paul Saffo, of the Institute for the Future, a California think tank, draws an intriguing parallel between the organizational structures of today's agile, customer-first organizations and the very technology those organizations are using to deliver results. "The organization of General Motors in the 1960s was a complex analog of a mainframe computer," he notes. "In this era, the model organization mirrors our networked information structure. It's a web, not a hierarchy. The big difference: In a hierarchy, your title determines your power. In a web, it's who you know." The shift in emphasis carries some significant implications indeed for executive assistants, who work with the most important players in the organization.

Frequently the executive assistant is the person who must determine which updates from the front and proposed new initiatives are worth immediate review by top executives. Correct decisions on this score can carry immense implications for the effort to carry out the organization's mission.

The Executive Assistant Must Act as Facilitator of Internal Renewal and Good Corporate Citizenship

Executive assistants can, and I believe should, play an important role in one of the most important ongoing changes of the new economy: the drive to attain diversity in the workforce to benefit both the corporation and society. Executive assistants may be the best positioned to realize the hidden talents of culturally varied employees.

Untapped ability is an awe-inspiring thing when it is pointed in the proper direction. There is an abundance of untapped ability in our society. Continuing their work as the eyes and ears of key decision makers, executive assistants will be at the forefront of diversity efforts, community outreach plans, and innovative human resource and training ideas that will help the workers of tomorrow develop their own talents and abilities. The accent throughout will be on accountability and personal and group responsibility. These are all initiatives executive assistants will promote, not merely because these efforts are worthwhile in the abstract, but also because they will further the strategic, profit-first aims of the successful twenty-first century corporation.

We are a nation of many cultures, and different cultures develop different ways of dealing with important issues. In today's web-style work groups, varying viewpoints can be a significant corporate advantage in assessing problems and challenges.

In a 1993 study at the University of Texas, the output of teams of ethnically diverse business students were quietly compared with those of all-white teams for 17 weeks. The racially homogeneous teams took an early lead, but by the end of the study the racially mixed teams were showing a greater aptitude for viewing problems from a variety of perspectives and were producing the most innovative solutions to the dilemmas they faced.

Among the corporate giants making diversity pay off in the real world is Motorola, the largest employer in the state of Arizona, which has instituted an aggressive diversity training and recruiting program since 1989. The company has invested $200 million in its diversity program since it was launched. Vice president Roberta Gutman says the main goal of the company's diversity efforts is to "get the best and the brightest minds in the world to come to Motorola." She points to admirable growth in a competitive field as one sign that the initiative is paying off.

Executive assistants, particularly those who are members of minority groups, can play important roles in helping to institute formal or informal mentoring policies for minorities in their organizations. Global companies such as Federal Express,

AT&T, and General Electric have all instituted or encouraged such internal minority-to-minority career assistance.

Ellis Cose, author of *The Rage of a Privileged Class,* put it this way: "It is going to be awfully hard to forge a globally competitive workforce if the races can't learn to work together." She's quite correct; fortunately, however, we *can* learn to work together, and to do so to the benefit of our organizations and our own careers. In the new economy the executive assistant is going to play a key role in helping make that happen.

The Executive Assistant Must Develop Competence in the Face of Ambiguity

Part of succeeding in the new economy is being comfortable with a business world marked by ambiguity, uncertainty, and constant reinvention. A sense of balance, and even excitement, amidst the turmoil of unexpected developments is essential. We should be prepared to see the excitement first, and the panic second.

The organization's "big picture" is subject to constant, and perhaps slightly bewildering, revision. Hoping that picture won't change is bound to lead us to failure and disappointment. Helping it change profitably and productively is what will lead us to fulfillment and growth. Often the executive assistant will be the first to realize that a course correction is necessary in the first place!

In the midst of all this ambiguity, however, one thing is certain. In addition to technology, the businesses of the twenty-first century are still going to require people. They will need people who are capable of harnessing the new technologies, people who can master the new and sometimes unfamiliar terrain of the hypercharged workplace. Businesses will need, in short, people who are comfortable with the notion of technological change *as a constant factor in their jobs.* Those who will be left out in the cold will be the ones who try to resist that change or who imagine it will not affect the way they work.

What is the alternative but to welcome the sweeping technological changes to come? And who is in a better position to benefit from the new, change-as-a-way-of-working-life mindset than the adept executive assistant?

The changes under way and shortly to come will demand that we learn to be comfortable with a working life lived on the "competitive edge"—a working life in which exploration, growth, and constant self-improvement and self-mastery are features of our daily routine.

Because the organization must find ways to accommodate the tidal waves of technological change it faces, we must find ways to adapt. We must develop the willingness to react, not with panic but with a sense of adventure akin to the entrepreneur's, to the new circumstances we will face on a daily basis. (And by the way, that "edge" where we will be spending so much of our time is also the place where companies will develop the profits that allow them to continue operation! Not a bad place to be at all.)

UNPARALLELED OPPORTUNITY FOR THOSE WHO EMBRACE CHANGE

In The Age of Social Transformation, Peter Drucker writes that we have entered a new age, one in which the jobs on the horizon will require continuous learning and willingness to change. Those who welcome change and continuous learning lead the most dynamic lives. In such an environment, you don't "hold onto" a job—you relentlessly prepare youself for an ever-wider range of opportunities.

Standing still is the only sin. Significant rewards await those who summon their courage and cross the stream.

Such as?

In all likelihood, the executive assistant's role will include both the *assessment* and the *implementation* of incredibly powerful new technologies for the organizations of the future. *We* will be the first to take advantage of the dramatic technological innovations taking place—and that will make *us* some of the most indispensable people in the entire structure.

We will play a central role in shepherding key players

through the pains and opportunities of the ongoing business information revolution. And in a lean-budget era when training funds are often minimal (or even nonexistent), *we* will become a vital resource for the top executives who will be expected to accomplish more with smaller staffs.

We will be in the first wave of team players who know *how to make the new machine do what it's supposed to do!* That's a keystone for career growth if there ever was one.

As a result of all this, and as a result of our own willingness to constantly ask ourselves how we can better adapt to new situations, we will find that "executive decisions" are often, at least in part, "administrative decisions" as well. Talk about opportunity!

But that opportunity will come at a cost. In today's business environment, we will have to take charge of our own development if we want to grow, or even keep up! It is not enough simply to deepen the skills we currently have. We must keep a watchful eye on our ability to make contributions in new areas, areas we may not yet know much about.

If we commit to becoming part of the group of people who can do that—one of the adapters—we will find that the earth-shaking technological changes to come are nothing to be afraid of. Instead, we will find that we are the ones who help key team members during both crisis and opportunity.

Though the times ahead may be a little jarring now and then, they nevertheless promise to be exhilarating ones in which to live. And at those moments when the ride gets a little bumpy, we can comfort ourselves with the thought that heading forward, even with the occasional jolt, beats going backward hands down.

CHAPTER FIVE

LEADING-EDGE COMMUNICATION SKILLS

No man would listen to you talk if he didn't know it was his turn next.

E. W. Howe

Appropriate communication skills, as we've seen, constitute a critical part of the executive assistant's job. In this chapter, we'll look at some of the most important talents you must possess when it comes to interacting with others.

DEFINING—AND MEETING—THE ONGOING REQUIREMENTS OF THE JOB

Knowing what is occurring in the organization, and by extension, knowing what information to pass along and how to pass it on to others, are fundamental requirements of the executive assistant's job. Verbal skills, including a solid mastery of vocabulary, are essential, as is excellence in written communication, including spelling, grammar, and proofreading. A good many executive assistants these days compose correspondence for their managers; virtually all have to handle some form of dictation or tape transcription. Exemplary computer skills, of course, are also a must.

You'll find here a brief overview of the basic communication skills you will need to meet the demands that face an executive assistant, along with suggestions based on the on-the-job situations that require your use of these skills. Of course, each job and each day present a host of new situations; hard-and-fast rules about what will be required with regard to communication will be less helpful than a commitment to revise your approach, and to redefine your goals, as new needs arise.

It's worth noting, too, that the deceptively simple term *communication* actually encompasses a vast horizon of meaning. Informing, confirming, persuading, mutually assessing, mutually prioritizing, and knowing when to withdraw and what *not* to focus on—these are all important parts of verbal and written communication in today's office environment. For that matter, so is developing a set of *global* communication skills that will allow you to account for cultural and ethnic factors as you help your manager avoid misunderstandings and blind alleys.

And these are by no means the only pieces of the puzzle. Mastering good communication skills, like so much of the work that falls to the contemporary executive assistant, is more of an ongoing process than an objective with a clear beginning, middle, and end.

There are, however, some quantifiable aspects to our workplace communication efforts, and those are covered in detail here. I strongly suggest that you take the tests that we administer at The Duncan Group (they appear in Appendix III) before you apply for a job as an executive assistant—and indeed, before you apply for any job that points you toward the executive assistant's position later on in your career. By testing yourself, you'll be able to determine problem areas as well as identify your strongest skills.

VERBAL COMMUNICATION

No matter how solid your technical skills or how impressive your level of knowledge about the target organization, your candidacy for an executive assistant's position will be diminished by poor verbal skills.

This position, you must remember, is one in which you will be performing a series of important duties independently and also *representing* your manager to others inside and outside the organization. That means that clear, effective communication is crucial. The manner in which you express yourself, just as much as the things you say, will influence how you are perceived by others, starting with the person who is interviewing you for the executive assistant's job! Some applicants with letter-perfect credentials find it difficult to get beyond the face-to-face interview stage for an executive assistant position; in a good number of cases, perhaps the majority, this is traceable to poor verbal skills, which may include inappropriate speech patterns, vocabulary problems, and other obstacles.

It is beyond the scope of this book to offer a review of all the techniques available to you for (1) improving your speaking style and (2) improving your face-to-face interactions with your manager (and, by extension, with others in the office). However, space does permit a discussion of some key strategies for enhancing your performance in these areas.

10 TIPS FOR IMPROVING YOUR VOCAL DELIVERY

All the following advice is likely to require sustained effort, perhaps over a period of weeks or months, before resulting in change. Practice makes perfect!

- Vary your tone. A relentless monotone is difficult to listen to and is very likely to cancel out your message entirely. Try this experiment. Tape-record 30 seconds or so of your own speech—assume you're formulating a series of status reports for your manager—and then record 30 seconds of the speech of a television newscaster from one of the nightly network broadcasts. Compare the two. You will, I'll bet, notice an easy gliding change in the cadences of the broadcaster. If your own speech doesn't naturally incorporate the same gentle, inviting up-and-down alterations of the broadcaster's—and it probably won't—practice daily until your speech comes closer to the million-dollar standard. That's the standard to employ when relating important information for your boss, information that's meant to hold the attention of others. Note: *Any* number of CEOs may be able to get away with a one-note, rat-a-tat vocal delivery. It is a rare aspiring executive assistant who is able to do so, however!

- Don't vary your tone in the wrong way. No, this is not a direct contradiction to the last piece of advice. What's at issue here is the extremely irritating habit of ending all, or nearly all, of your sentences on an upward lilt, as though you were about to ask a question.
- Slow down. Most of us talk faster than we realize. If you need to switch to decaf in order to ask questions and relay information in a nonintimidating manner, make the switch! Again, tape-recording your own speech is a good idea for self-monitoring exercises on this score.
- Practice incessantly to eliminate verbal rough spots that make your speech sound too informal. By these I mean not only such obvious problems as dropping the final *g* off of words like *inviting,* but also heavy regional influences that are likely to lead others to assume that you are less intelligent than you are. It is certainly true that erasing such deeply imbedded speech patterns is often a long-term project; you should know, though, that the best jobs usually go to the people who *do* overcome verbal stereotyping. Make a commitment to learn how to present a polished, attractive verbal image free from regional influence. (By the way, reading out loud is a great way to overcome pronunciation and diction problems.)
- Enunciate crisply and correctly. Don't cheat words out of consonants that belong to them or introduce new ones into places they don't belong. This, too, may take some practice, since long-standing habit and the influence of friends and relatives may have convinced you that the word *pattern* does not contain an *r* sound, or that the word *idea* does contain an *r* sound at the end. If necessary, enlist the aid of a friend—preferably one who does not share your precise speech pattern—to offer constructive criticism.
- Speak up. Don't expect to build a good relationship with a top decision maker by mumbling. If you're uncertain about something, state your uncertainty in a confident, certain way!

- Breathe from your diaphragm. Shallow breathing is a sign of inadequately developed vocal potential. A good Broadway actor can't afford to indulge in this practice, and neither can you. Breathing correctly not only will improve your speech patterns, but will also help you center yourself and deal more effectively with stressful situations.
- Don't be afraid to stop talking. Yes, there is certainly something to be said for filling an awkward conversational hole with the occasional piece of social fluff. But you are likely to increase your level of personal stress—and steadily decrease your own verbal precision—when you repeat the same points over and over again. Knowing when the message is finished is just as much an art as knowing when and how to send it.
- Watch those dangerous consonants. If pronouncing a word with a *p* or an *s* is likely to leave your conversational partner reaching for a handkerchief, you need to work on the clarity of your speech, or try to choose words that present less difficulty.
- Adapt the volume of your voice to the level of your conversational partner. When dealing with your manager, you don't want to make the mistake of seeming to shout him or her down!

10 Tips for Improving Your Face-to-Face Interactions with Others

All the ideas for improving one-on-one interactions that follow are offered with the assumption that you will be dealing with your boss. This makes sense, since he or she is likely to be the person with whom you have the most—and the most important—contact during the course of a given day. It's worth noting, however, that showing the same respect, attentiveness, precision, and concern that are reflected in the following ideas is also sound strategy when dealing with people at all levels of the organization. It's encouraging how people who listen to those both above *and* below them on the organizational chart have a tendency to rise on that very chart!

- Repeat important messages back to show your manager—and yourself!—that they've been heard and understood. This is infinitely preferable to nodding your head vigorously in an attempt to convince your manager that you understand something fully. Let's face it; often we *don't* understand, even when we nod our heads and think that we do! What would such a repeated message sound like? Perhaps like this: "Okay, so I have four things on the list for this morning: confirm the date and time of the Los Angeles flight, summarize the key points of that *Wall Street Journal* article and submit it to you for an okay before passing it along to the rest of the staff, call and remind your wife about your dinner date with her tonight, and order 16 copies of the new draft of the speech you'll be giving in Los Angeles."

  Once you've reviewed all the key ideas *as your manager has laid them out for you,* you will be looking for a confirming message ("That sounds like everything") or additional input ("Did I say 16? I'm sorry; we're only going to need 12 copies of this speech"). *Repeating messages back in this way is one of the most important talents of sound communicators.* When you review, responsibly and without the slightest trace of sarcasm, all your conversational partner's key points, you open the gates that allow for a fruitful exchange of information. It is usually at this point, and not before, that you find the other person is open to the messages *you* may need to pass along.

- Answer questions directly. Effective decision makers learn quickly who will handle the tough issues head on, and who is likely to dodge or obfuscate when faced with a difficult inquiry. It is an undeniable fact of the executive assistant's life that the boss is likely, on occasion, to pose questions that whoosh ahead like heat-seeking missiles in search of accountable parties. Harsh, impatient, or even tactless questions are one thing. Do you really have to look straight ahead, directly into the line of fire, when your manager unloads a question that seems aimed only at establishing who is to blame? Yes. The virtue of accountability is one that cannot be overemphasized in the modern executive assistant; learning to accept responsibility and/or admit a knowledge gap is an essential skill, especially in today's "flattened" organizations where the manager may have only one person to hold accountable for anything! No one is suggesting that you must routinely accept responsibility for the mistakes or oversights of others; at the same time, you should be aware of the predisposition of decisive people to get to the bottom of things in a hurry. Work with that predisposition; offer intelligent assessments of the current situation, even assessments that don't make you look very good, before you fall back on excuses or double-talk.

- Don't be afraid to quote the other person as an authority. Think about how *you'd* feel if your manager said to you, "I was thinking the other day of what you said last week about the importance of assigning multiple proofreaders to important documents *before* we get hit with a serious error. I think you were absolutely right, and I mentioned that to the rest of the team this morning during a staff meeting." You would feel marvelous, wouldn't you? Your manager will feel just the same when you cite an on-target observation that has helped you make sense of your own workday. When you find something useful in a remark of your manager's, something that you've been able to adopt to your benefit on a regular basis, say so. A relationship built on mutual trust and respect allows for these exchanges. The good feelings you generate will encourage a unique bond between you and your manager and may help encourage an open dialogue when you offer tactfully phrased suggestions on other matters.
- When in doubt, let your boss have the credit for ideas you discuss together. This is a simple, reliably successful rule for avoiding tense interactions later on down the line, a rule that needs little or no elucidation. If you've hooked up with the type of person who is likely to take advantage of you for following this principle—by, for instance, underpaying you or short-circuiting your career growth—try to find another person for whom to work. But my experience is that such bosses, while not unheard of, are the exception, not the rule in the team-first organization. You're there to help your boss

get things done, not to take the lead role away from him or her. If you regularly feel the need to occupy the spotlight, you may be in the wrong job.

- Be willing to admit you were wrong. This is an essential ability. Your boss may not possess it (a good many high-powered types don't), in which case it is all the more vital that you do.
- Know when to back off. Just because something is at the top of your list does not mean it occupies a similarly prominent position on your manager's agenda. Sometimes *nothing* will occupy the most prominent position on your manager's agenda. Sometimes that's essential. Today's technology—laptops, e-mail systems, voicemail, and so on—allow access to extraordinary amounts of information. They also lead a good many important executives to a daily period of "information burnout," a half-hour or more at the end of the day during which normal human communication is problematic. There's a good chance your boss will fall into this category and that he or she will dismiss a seemingly critical initiative with disturbing nonchalance and the strange, glassy-eyed stare of someone who's simply been exposed to too many facts during too brief a period of time. Unless you're facing a true crisis situation, which is unlikely, you should not press your manager for action during this period. Try again later.
- Offer a completion date before you're asked for one. Highly efficient people tend to divide the world up into two types of people: those, like themselves, who set deadlines independently, and those who don't. Be sure that you fall into the former category.
- Use humor to put your boss at ease. The right kind of humor—refreshing and irreverent but never inappropriate or tactless—will go a long way toward establishing the right emotional climate between yourself and your boss. Humor is a strange thing; what one person finds on target may strike another as bewildering or even threatening. Don't be surprised if it takes you a little time to develop a working, shared sense of humor with your boss. Once you do, however, you will probably find that you can appeal to it even—

especially!—during times when you and your boss are facing a challenging situation together.

- Ask for more time when you need it. Your boss will usually have a bigger problem with a series of missed deadlines than with a single, forthright, accurate request for more time. On your own initiative, put the request in writing and then hit the mark. (Use of e-mail technology can be a big plus on this front.)
- Is there a sudden crisis at hand? Offer options and suggest solutions, not problems, when you report it to your boss. This is one of the most important verbal communication skills of them all. It deserves to be addressed in some depth, and so I'm going to discuss it in detail here.

You and your boss possess a relationship that exists, at least ideally, in a mutually complementary union of talents. This union is one in which each person fills in certain gaps for the other, and both work in harmony to develop creative solutions to the problems that arise unexpectedly. It follows that you, if not always your boss, must approach even serious setbacks, obstacles, and adversities as *shared* challenges, rather than as the problem of one or the other person. This eliminates from consideration two possible responses to a troublesome state of affairs: (1) admitting that something has slipped past you, and throwing yourself on the mercy of your boss, which leaves him or her responsible for deciding what to do next; or (2) dumping the problem in your boss's lap, which leaves him or her responsible for deciding what to do next.

Once you cross these two options off the roster of actions available to you, you'll have only one left—assuming a fair share of responsibility for the situation in which you and your boss find yourselves, and offering intelligent choices for him or her to consider or build upon. I suggest that you make a habit of supplying at least three. In almost all cases these must be choices you flesh out and consider fully, rather than rash applications of the rule book to whatever set of facts may be staring you in the face. I say "almost all cases" because I know of a good many executive assistants who have adapted the three-options rule to noncrisis situations as a way of encouraging dilatory bosses to make decisions! Have some idea of the potential ramifications of your options, and *briefly* state all the alternatives you've discovered and their attendant possible effect on circumstances *immediately after you outline the problem for your boss.* Today's effective executive assistants don't dump—they self-manage and think! Thinking is a prerequisite to reporting *any* crisis situation to your boss. Even if the choices you describe turn out not to be the best ways to proceed with the problem at hand, you may well inspire a creative approach that is.

WRITTEN COMMUNICATION SKILLS

As many an observant social critic has noted, the technological revolution that placed personal computers on our desks and offered us access to the information superhighway failed spectacularly to fulfill its promise to deliver unto us a paper-free office. The appearance of e-mail and file transfer systems seems to have had the effect of rendering us *more* reliant on the printed word than was the case 20 years ago, because people invariably want multiple hard copies of key pieces of correspondence!

All this is by way of noting that solid writing and associated presentation skills remain essentials for the capable executive assistant. Most assistants must compose text for their bosses; virtually all must oversee the development of important documents. If you feel your ability to set things down on paper or into an electronic data retrieval system needs improving, here are some ideas that may be helpful.

- Whenever possible, keep written communication to one page with bullet points. People—especially busy people—tend to ignore or zip through messages that run for longer than a single page or screenful of data. Of course, not everything that has to be communicated can be consolidated into a single page. But believe it or not, the vast majority can, even if that means alerting your boss to a briefly summarized emergency that requires an immediate face-to-face meeting! You say you can't get the information your boss needs into a single page? Try harder. David Mamet's play *Speed the Plow* features a great line about story summaries for movie screenplays that illustrates the point to perfection. One of Mamet's Hollywood producer types says to another of his Hollywood producer types something akin to the following: "If you can't tell me what the movie's about in a single sentence, they can't list it in *TV Guide!*"

- Use quotes from outside sources to support your points. Did you notice how the previous piece of advice, about writing concisely, gained impact as a result of its incorporating an anecdote of external origin—the remark from the David Mamet play? Invest in a good paperback collection of quotes. Then, when you're running dry, take a few moments to dip into the collection to find a quote you can use and attribute properly in your memo or report. (You should also make a habit of reading voraciously—both materials that relate directly to your job and those that don't, such as the op-ed pieces in your local paper.) By using quotes appropriately you'll not only spice up your writing, you'll probably illuminate some new aspect of your topic that you had not previously considered. Perhaps the quote you cite can lead your writing in a profitable new direction.
- Banish "writer's block": part I. Keep a phrase file. This is a file of those observations, ideas, brainstorms, and other gems you can't fit into the project you're working on at the moment. Jot these down in a notebook; appeal to it when you need a compelling new idea to liven up a document. Perhaps all-new ideas arising from a cited quote you use in another document, as discussed above, can be profitably entered into your phrase file. Sometimes the best way to cure a case of so-called writer's block—an imaginary disease if there ever was one—is to head back into the phrase file and see what gems are waiting to be reset for the world to admire.
- Banish "writer's block": part II. Do something else! The single most effective way to overcome the much-lamented

"blank paper syndrome" is, thankfully, also the easiest. Stop trying to force yourself to be brilliant—it's impossible to force yourself to be brilliant—and look away from your project for a moment or two. Count the ceiling tiles in the office. Sing a song to yourself. Make a phone call. Give yourself 2 minutes to focus on a mindless, routine aspect of some other project, and then get back to your document! Your mind is ready, willing, and eager to point you in the right direction on the project at hand—but your mind is ornery. It may need to be distracted for just a brief moment so that it can believe it came up with the idea of being amazingly creative all on its own. So distract it. Don't lecture it. I like to keep a big glass of water at hand near my desk. When I'm writing and I hit a roadblock, I take seven, and only seven, sips of the water. After the seventh calm, focused sip, I return to the job at hand. The roadblock always disappears!

- Attentively read *The Elements of Style* by Strunk and White, making notes as you go along. Then read it again. Then keep it by your side at all times and make a commitment to follow its sage advice whenever you write. If you follow these three simple instructions, you will be miles ahead of the competition when it comes to crafting clear, concise, comprehensible documents. Even in an era of extraordinary organizational and technological change, some things remain ageless. *The Elements of Style* is one of them.
- Use written communications to save your boss, or anyone else, the time it takes to follow up. When you complete an important task, either make a photocopy of the memo that brought the task to your attention, or compose a brief "completion" memo of your own that alerts your boss to the status of the project in question. Keep and file copies of everything.
- Use headlines! Especially when time is tight—and when isn't it in the modern office? The people who get your message want to be able to review it in a matter of seconds, not minutes. That means you will be doing your reader and yourself a favor if you compose a short, catchy initial sentence that captures the essence of your document. Some examples:

"Travel agent says deadline for purchasing Chicago tickets is this Friday!" "Late nights may be necessary to complete the catalog on time—shall I circulate an overtime schedule?" "Emergency update from the printer: The books have been delayed until the 24th!" After a line like one of these, you can proceed to the details of the message in the rest of your document. The headline rule is particularly important to follow if you decide, for some unfathomable reason, to make a habit of ignoring the one-page rule outlined above in your day-to-day work. If you must create multipage documents, be sure they are broken up into appropriate sections that begin with an eye-grabbing headline.

- Take some time to select your fonts with care. Today's word processing systems allow you to add impact to your documents in ways that few people other than typesetters and graphic artists would have dreamed of 10 years ago. And yet, a document crowded with too *many* different looks or without any sense of proportion is probably harder to read than something pumped out of an IBM Selectric. Your best bet is to invest a very little up-front time to select two *complementary yet contrasting* typefaces—perhaps a dramatic face for headlines and chapter titles such as Impact, and good old Times Roman, or whatever variation on it shows up on your word processing system, for body text. With just a little initial effort, you can set up a word processing template that allows you to *automatically* shift between the two faces and add power and dynamism to your printed materials. Whatever you do, *don't* overload your documents with seven or eight typefaces, or colors, for that matter, vying for dominance on a single page. All you'll do is make people's eyes hurt. (*Note:* It may seem superficial to devote much attention to such questions as type selection and balance in your written documents, but you may rest assured that memos people actually *read* are far more effective than memos they don't!) The most painstakingly crafted one-page memo you've ever composed will be for naught if it doesn't intelligently distinguish body text from headline, or if it seems to be hosting a tag-team match for an incongruous collection of fonts.

- Don't trust yourself; ask someone else to look the work over. On documents of above-average importance—for instance, communications to shareholders, responses to members of the news media, and press releases—a single pair of eyes is not enough. Find someone else who has the time to help you review critical written communications before they go out to the important people who'll be reading them. And while we're on the topic of double-checking things…
- Don't trust spell-checking programs! In the chapter concerning the job search, I made mention of the importance of human proofreading, rather than a machine check, of your résumé and cover letter. The point is just as important on the job. No, you don't have to set up multiple-participant proofreading and style checklists for the everyday correspondence you share with your colleagues or subordinates. By the same token, do not, under any circumstances assume that a document spell-checked only by computer is free of errors and ready for review by the Powers That Be. Remember: Accuracy and detail orientation are the workplace passions of an effective executive assistant.

IS THAT IT?

Well, no. We could spend a whole book addressing the best ways to handle the hazards and opportunities of effective interpersonal communication in the workplace. But the ideas above are a good starting place. If you remember only one principle from the above discussion, make it this one:

> *Take responsibility for the challenges and obstacles you and your manager face by listening and by making the commitment to develop and present concrete, intelligent options for dealing with those challenges.*

As we've discussed, the successful executive in today's work environment is one who has much more in common with the entrepreneur than she does with the filing clerk. Entrepreneurs don't have any choice; they *have* to take responsibility and be intuitive decision makers when they face unfortunate situations.

I'll let you in on a secret: After a while they learn that it's actually quite fulfilling to do so. For too many years our society fostered a style of "corporate communication" that evaded responsibility as much as it embraced it, and clouded meaning and intention more than it illuminated them. If we could ever afford to engage in that type of communication, we certainly can't now.

Take responsibility, and say you're taking responsibility, even when the chips are down. Present specific options. Listen. Ask questions that open doors, rather than shut them. If you do all this, you'll be in a good position to develop a sound, productive set of communication patterns with your boss and with others in the organization.

What to Do When Communications Are Deteriorating

What happens if you follow all the advice in this chapter, and you still find yourself in a situation where you and your boss appear to be speaking in entirely different languages? The short answer: *Stop talking and take notes.*

Taking notes, as premier sales trainer Stephan Schiffman has pointed out in his lectures and seminars, is the single best way to get communications back on the right track. When you stop talking, pull out a pencil and a pad of paper, look intently at the other person, and ask what that person thinks should happen next—bingo! You're talking that person's language! Write everything down, and don't interrupt with questions. Save those for later on, when your manager, or whomever else you're trying to get in sync with, has exhausted the topic.

By following this approach, you eliminate the possibility of your conversational partner thinking you hope to exercise some kind of power play during the conversation (which you don't, right?). You also leave yourself with a detailed record of the subject under discussion.

Take notes and ask appropriate questions. That's the short answer to the what-do-I-do-when-we-can't-seem-to-communicate question. For variations on any number of longer answers, see the ideas in Chapter 7, which focuses on conflict resolution.

CHAPTER SIX

LEADING-EDGE LEADERSHIP AND MANAGEMENT SKILLS

I suppose that leadership at one time meant muscle, but today it means getting along with people.

—Indira Gandhi

From resolving urgent telephone calls from a branch office to coordinating early-morning team meetings when the boss is delayed, today's executive assistant is called upon more and more to display tact, judgment, precision, and the ability to help others get things done. Here are some ideas on how to help pick up the slack for your boss when it comes to dealing effectively with other people in the organization.

WHEN YOU SPEAK FOR THE BOSS

It should come as no surprise to learn that many of today's leaner, more flexible organizations have a habit of leaving people feeling spread pretty thin. If you're an executive assistant, it's a pretty good bet that your boss is going to be one of those people and that you'll be asked to work things out in any number of situations where your boss will be unable or unwilling to do so.

This does *not* mean, however, that you've earned the right to act capriciously or insensitively toward other team members! If you do so, your excesses will reflect badly not only on you, but also on your boss. When you act on behalf of an important executive, your job is both easier and more difficult than that of the executive. It's *easier* because you can and should make it clear at all points of your interaction with others that you are not pursuing a personal agenda, but carrying out the broad instructions you've received from your boss. This takes much of the ego investment out of the situation, and it may help you gain consensus in ways that someone who is acting independently cannot. The job is more *difficult*, however, because your own authority is limited, and you won't be able to resolve every question or crisis that comes up.

In other words, you must strike a balance—and do so as a surrogate, one who is scrupulously attentive to the repercussions of her words and actions. I spoke earlier in the book about the executive assistant's being denied the right to pound the table during a tense discussion. That goes double—triple?—for times when you must represent your boss at internal meetings, or supervise others in his or her name.

That's all very well, you may be thinking, but how exactly do I go about getting others to *do* something my boss wants them to do? Five strategies on this score follow.

FIVE STRATEGIES FOR EFFECTIVE WORK WITH TEAMS WHO LOOK TO YOU FOR LEADERSHIP

- Use quantifiable targets. Exhorting others to "show attention to detail" or "make that extra effort" may make *you* feel better, but it won't do much to help the people you're working with progress toward a goal. Summarize the task at hand so that it is expressed in terms of some *measurable* output. Involve the team in planning the steps to completion; create a shared-effort environment. Yes, this all can be done even when you're dealing with a so-called objective task. ("Mr. Jones wants to develop some new ideas for the cover of the fall catalog; please take some time this morning to develop at least five different possible design approaches. Don't try to execute them completely; just focus on setting up at least five sketches.")

- Offer periodic feedback and support. Simply issuing an instruction isn't enough. Make an effort to follow up and monitor the progress people are making, and when you see someone carrying out more or less what you and your boss had in mind, praise the person for the effort. Praise—especially *public* praise—is one of the most powerful motivators at your disposal.
- Provide examples, rather than speaking in terms of vague ideals, when trying to help someone improve. Is there a previous project or assignment you can point to, one that was completed in the right way? By calling attention to it, you will be able to help point your team members in the right direction, and you'll probably inspire the person whose work you've praised to achieve even greater heights.
- Put it in writing. No, a written memo isn't a *replacement* for intelligent face-to-face coaching, but it's often an invaluable *addition* to it. By setting out goals clearly, concisely, and sensitively in a single one-page memo, you will save time, lessen the possibility of error, and lessen the likelihood of miscommunication. See the ideas outlined in Chapter 5.
- Listen to the team. Is there a flashing red light that you and your boss should know about? Don't be too eager to dismiss those objections or stumbling blocks people bring to your attention. You're standing in for your boss not simply to issue instructions, but also to report on new situations and opportunities that arise. One of the very best ways to win the loyalty of the team with which you're working is to prove you're willing to listen to all legitimate concerns, and pass them on to the boss for review without divulging confidences. Make sure your organization's team-oriented thinking—which is probably what landed you in this short-term managerial situation in the first place—is a reality, not just a slogan.

YOUR UNIQUE ROLE AS TEAM LEADER: DEFINING OBJECTIVES AND MAKING THE MOST OF SUGGESTED CHANGES

An executive assistant in a formal or informal managerial situation is a common sight in this team-first era. Make the most of this opportunity and of your own status as a resident of both the power center and the working group. *Pass along the good ideas you hear!*

Yes, your boss is busy. Yes, you are supposed to help execute the specific initiative that has been entrusted to you. Yes, you must be sensitive to your boss's tight schedule. But you are also the eyes and ears of your boss, and that means passing along and crediting intelligent new approaches when they arise under your watch.

Herewith some ideas for helping make sure a good idea shows up on your boss's radar screen—without too badly disrupting that carefully crafted schedule you've set up.

- Quote a customer. If one of the members of your team has an important piece of market intelligence to pass along from the front line, one that may necessitate a change of strategy, consider asking the team member to set the information down in the form of a brief (and accurate) written quote from one of your organization's customers. Then pass it along to your boss and see what happens.
- Schedule a 10-minute meeting between your boss and the team. For some executives the very beginning of the day is the best time to handle this type of meeting, in which the team members are asked to *briefly* summarize their important update or proposed change in strategy. By the way, have you ever noticed how more tends to get done during meetings with strictly enforced time limits than during long, rambling ones? It's something to consider mentioning the next time your manager starts lamenting about all the time spent in drawn-out group sessions.
- Try doing things the way the team is suggesting for a short trial period, then report the (good) results to your boss and

ask for permission to proceed in the same manner. Clearly, you'll want to be fairly sure about the merit of the idea being proposed, as well as the manageability of the possible downside of your trial run. If the idea in question has the potential to hurt your organization's reputation, eat up massive amounts of people's time, or tear a budget to shreds, then you should probably take a pass on this option. If you feel confident that there's a decent chance for success and see little or no risk of running into a productivity, expense, or public relations quagmire, then you may want to consider letting the team try out its idea on a small scale. If the results are strong and seem likely to deliver when extrapolated out to a larger setting, you will probably want to summarize the experiment for your boss in a single-page memo and ask for input and/or permission to proceed along the lines of the team's suggestion.

HOW TO HANDLE A CRISIS

Horrors! Something's gone wrong with the team you've been supervising! Is it time to panic?

Of course not. Remember, the very nature of the executive assistant's job is to deal with crises of one kind or another. No matter how badly things have gone, *you must maintain the same poise necessary if you were coordinating a problem for your boss.* Sit down with the team and develop an intelligent assessment of exactly what's happened. Don't be misled by emotional reports of catastrophe—they're usually inaccurate. Focus on the facts, and break them down into hard numbers whenever you can. (You'll be committing all this information into a single-page summary for your boss.)

Then ask for your team's input on developing *three workable responses to the crisis you face.* The worse the situation, the more nominees you'll need to consider for the final three, but don't get sidetracked by minutiae. Keep your team talking. Write all the ideas down on a flipchart, blackboard, or large sheet of paper visible to all the team members. Doing this helps inspire group creativity. Write down every idea, no matter how absurd. Don't rule anything out; if you do, you may discourage people from offering unorthodox suggestions.

Once you've settled on the three best options, commit both the summary of the problem and your three proposed recommendations to paper—one page maximum—and pass it along to your boss.

It bears repeating here that a certain calmness within—and an ability to predict the course of—the storm is essential for this job. I have yet to meet the successful executive assistant who hasn't cultivated the ability to think clearly during a crisis. Don't freeze. Don't panic. Take a deep breath and look at the best options you and your inherited work group face. Then bring your boss up to speed on the latest turn of events and explain how you'd take action.

SOME FINAL THOUGHTS ON THE LEADERSHIP ROLE

Leadership means, among other things, summoning the ability to cope with and bring about change. That is to say, true leadership may be thought of as the art of not quitting when something unexpected happens.

Leadership means being an empathetic listener. Listening sensitively is difficult, because when we allow ourselves to see the world through another's eyes and to fully understand his or her point of view, we run the risk of changing our point of view, and ourselves. But it is only through listening that we develop and maintain close relationships, in which there is enough freedom to express feelings and observations honestly. In *The Seven Habits of Highly Effective People,* Stephen R. Covey writes, "(W)hen I say empathetic listening, I mean listening with intent to understand...you are focused on receiving the deep communication of another human soul."

Leadership accepts chaos as an existing precondition, and doesn't struggle against it or attempt to resolve it instantly with short-term solutions. This may present a challenge to the order-conscious executive assistant. The temptation to resolve *all* problems, to systematize *all* situations, to incorporate structure *everywhere,* can be a strong one. But in some settings, deciding not to make a decision—yet—is the best possible option, the one that leaves the most alternatives open to you, your manager, and your organization.

Leadership means considering new approaches, keeping an eye on results, and being willing to refine things as time goes on. It also means being able to appeal to needs in order to inspire people to do what must be done. Leaders help others learn to deal with new systems and procedures; they also summon the experiences and insights of others in a constructive way that benefits the organization as a whole.

Not infrequently, leadership means making a commitment to personal growth and mastery. How else are you supposed to maintain poise in the face of chaos?

Leadership, when you are called upon to provide it (as more and more executive assistants are), is certainly exciting, but it can also be exhausting. It usually demands that you find the best solution with the tools available to you at the time, and that you do so in a manner that awakens the passions of others. It is an open-ended process in which "failure" requires more work (in order to address existing obstacles) and "success" requires more work (in order to bring about similarly positive outcomes in other areas). Once you show a knack for leadership, people have a way of knocking on your door again and again and asking you to take it on.

CHAPTER SEVEN

LEADING-EDGE CONFLICT RESOLUTION SKILLS

Trumpet in a herd of elephants; crow in the company of cocks; bleat in a flock of goats.

—Old Malaysian Proverb

Egos, self-interest, and insecurity are usually the biggest barriers to teamwork. Effective conflict resolution is often a matter of helping people stop fixating on these obstacles and begin putting their attention to work elsewhere. This is easier said than done, perhaps, but in this chapter we'll look at some of the best ways to accomplish the goal.

The truth is that people who work for very important top executives often have a relatively easy time resolving disputes among other team members. It's (usually) a given that team members try to act with uncommon grace, forbearance, tact, and understanding when they know you serve as the eyes and ears of the executive. You can use this to your advantage during stressful times by means of any number of discreet reminders about your status. Here are a few of my favorites.

How do you think Mr./Ms. Smith [i.e., your own manager] would handle this situation? (Translation: Step back and think about a new way to handle it. There are more options at your disposal than you think.)

I have to admit that this falls into a gray area for me. If your two teams can't resolve this problem on your own, I can't think of anything else to do other than ask Mr./Ms.

Smith how to proceed. (Translation: Do you want me to pass the details of this problem along, or can you resolve it creatively yourself?)

Mr./Ms. Smith didn't mention anything about this to me. (Translation: What you're suggesting seems to me to be out of bounds and would probably be treated as such by my manager. Can't you think up another way to attack this problem?)

No one is suggesting that you make a habit of employing such techniques in *all* of your encounters with people who seem to be at loggerheads. By the same token, judicious, nonthreatening, and delicately phrased reminders of the boss's trust in you can occasionally serve as spectacular tools for eliciting consensus and disrupting antagonistic communication patterns.

SEEING THROUGH OBSTACLES AND DEVELOPING A POSITIVE RELATIONSHIP WITH OTHERS

What other tools can you use to help put out fires around the office—a task that in today's flexibly arranged organizations may fall to you with greater frequency than ever? Here are 10 ideas that you can adapt profitably to team members at all levels of the organization, including your own boss.

- Disengage and take notes. See the advice on this technique in Chapter 5. Disengaging has the advantage of demonstrating *visually* to your conversational partner that you are in fact listening, which is the first and best way to resolve a conflict with a superior, a colleague, or a subordinate.
- Ask for time to think about a proposed course of action, and then excuse yourself from the conversation. This is the workplace equivalent of counting to 10. Follow up appropriately.
- Cornered by a rudenik who won't let you disengage? Ignore challenging questions or accusations; take a deep breath and focus on the plans you can make to deal with the current sit-

uation. Know where you want this discussion to end up; stick to your plan. In the best of cases involving rudeniks, attacks are launched when your conversational partner has had to deal with too many stressful situations in a row. In the worst of cases, attacks are launched when your conversational partner sees you as an enemy and is hoping to knock you off balance. In both situations, the challenging question or accusation is not to be mistaken with credible assessments of your value as a person. Of course, the same two principles hold for attacks launched upon a third party by your conversational partner. The truth of the matter is you can usually, not always but usually, move toward a responsible disposition of the conflict by letting the attacker vent his or her feelings. You can then proceed by offering practical, realistic suggestions. So don't interrupt. Don't contradict. Don't encourage more irresponsible remarks by offering rebuttals. Keep your poise. When the opportunity presents itself, outline the situation as you see it and present a plan for action.

- Identify common goals. It may be challenging, but in most conflicts you can build a bridge by emphasizing shared objectives. If you play your cards right, you may be able to make this task easier by using a handy rhetorical device that has a way of lessening the tension among disagreeing participants: restating messages to you. "The way I see it, you're saying that we want to be sure the project is executed to the highest possible level of quality. That's exactly how I feel about it, too." Once you've established a common objective, you may be in a better position to identify—tactfully, and with careful, open-ended questioning—the lines of responsibility that will help you attain that objective.
- Focus on quantifiable facts, not your impressions, memories, or opinions; then establish mutual benefits for arriving at agreed-upon outcomes. Have you ever noticed how a good many of the most intense arguments tend to turn on the most insignificant issues? What someone said or didn't say, whether someone does or doesn't have a particular attitude, whether something "always" or "never" happens. These are points that are rooted in memory, defensive rebuttal, and per-

ception, and they can vary amazingly from one person to the next. When we insist on making a perception the topic of discussion, we may help polarize an already tense situation. Stay away from generalizations that are rooted in your own experience, especially generalizations that leave the other person no way to respond other than to make an outright denial, such as "Your department always manages to mess up the schedule somehow." Focus on facts acceptable to everyone. ("We've got to find a way to make up a week in the schedule.") Be wary, however, of fixating on issues that deal with whether someone is or was "lying" or "misleading" another about a particular point. Successful conflict resolution is more likely to feature outcomes that allow for honorable exits; if there is no incentive to pursue such an exit, there will be little chance for a positive, constructive outcome to the dispute.

- Consider yielding on ego issues. People tend to dig in for the long haul when they feel that some personal challenge to their competence, or their status within the organization, has been issued. Therefore, don't issue such challenges if you can possibly avoid doing so. If you find yourself snared in a conflict in which the other person has a vested stake in being right, think through the implications of admitting that the other person *is* right. Will the project collapse? Will the roof cave in? Will you be able to stop arguing and get back to your work? In many, many, cases, the answers are no, no, and yes, respectively. And if you inherit a conflict in which someone else is issuing personal challenges, don't be afraid to engage in a little creative positivism as a tactic for removing the mutual insecurity. Let's face it: Flattery is popular for a reason. Judiciously used by a shrewd referee, it can leave both sides of an ego-driven confrontation feeling that they've won on what matters: their status and sense of self. Very often, you can override argument content by allowing the combatants to revel in areas of personal excellence. It leaves people feeling better about themselves and their work than otherwise, which counts for something.
- Don't forget that you've got a body and that it has an effect on the proceedings. We often overlook the fact that physical pos-

turing and positioning can have an extraordinary impact on conflict generation. Watch where (and how) you place yourself. Make a conscious effort to respect the personal space of others; be particularly careful about striding behind someone's desk to "offer a better look" at a memo, report, or news item. This innocent-seeming maneuver is in fact a direct invasion of the other person's territory and may very well be perceived consciously or subconsciously as a direct challenge. People don't think very clearly when this occurs, and your initial intent—offering more information to help illuminate a situation—may be lost in the adrenaline. Another body-positioning no-no involves facing down another person. Toe to toe and eye to eye means either "Wanna fight?" or "Wanna make whoopie?" in body-speak, and you don't want to send either message. Leave plenty of distance. Approach at an angle. Don't stare.

- Be sure your tone of voice matches your message. Our voices carry subjective intent messages as well as facts and opinions. *How* you say something turns out to be far, far more important than *what* you say. There are two ways to say, for instance, "I really hope we can get to the bottom of this; still, given the deadline on the Hughes project, I don't think we should focus on it right now":
  - If you wish to send your conversational partner the message that you share his or her concern about whatever issue you feel should take a back seat to the Hughes project, you'd accent the words in this way: "I *really* hope we can get to the bottom of this; still, given the deadline on the Hughes project, I don't think we should focus on it *right now.*"
  - If, on the other hand, you wanted your conversational partner to understand that you're sick and tired of hearing about yet another obstacle to the group's completing the Hughes project, and you don't particularly want to deal with any obstacles now or in the foreseeable future, you'd say this: "I really hope we can get to the bottom of this; still, *given the deadline on the Hughes project,* I *don't* think we should *focus* on it right now."

Say the two sentences out loud yourself with the varying accents—you'll hear the difference! The first message is likely to help you resolve the conflict in priorities that's arisen; the second is likely only to exacerbate it, because it contains an unspoken demand that your listener appreciate how polite you're being at not rejecting the idea of focusing on his or her concerns outright. Such mixed-message demands tend to bring about anger, overt or repressed, in the people to whom they're directed. If you're going to go to the trouble of saying something comforting, you might as well mean it. Otherwise, your listener will pick up on your insincerity, and the conflict will almost certainly escalate.

- Dealing with a high-level executive? Don't spend much time outlining the details of what you plan to do or what stands in the way of your doing what you plan to do. Be brief! Most important decision makers prefer to focus on the broad outlines, and they will start getting restless when they hear detailed technical summaries. In most cases, what people in this group want to hear is, "I'll make sure it gets taken care of," not "What we have to resolve before it gets done is..." Many conflicts arise from this language choice. If you find yourself caught up in a situation in which you seem to be speaking a different language from the one another person in authority expects to hear, change your presentation! An executive won't want to be lectured about the ins and outs of a complex technical procedure, or whether or not something that isn't working has been approved. Accept the other person's viewpoint rather than trying to fight it: focus on what's going to happen next.
- The same process applies to your interactions with administrative and support staff members, only in this situation the objective is often to *emphasize* detail. Part of your job is to help translate the broad objectives ("This proposal must be completed by Friday, and we have to be careful to incorporate all the notes from the most recent meeting") into tangible how-tos ("She wants to change the cover color from blue to red, and she wants the following text changes..."). If you find yourself in a conflict, it may be because you're not

being specific enough with the person who must turn a set of sweeping instructions into reality. Check to see if you're sending messages that focus too much on the big picture and not enough on the nitty-gritty details. Ask the person to repeat to you what you have said.

Make no mistake: Dealing with conflict is part of the executive assistant's daily life. By applying the ideas outlined above, you will be able to make an honest effort to resolve conflicts harmoniously, or at least rationally explore the pros and cons of the course of action your conversational partner is advocating. We may not be able to eliminate dissension from our day—it's probably unhealthy to think we can do so—but we can increase the odds that the conflicts we do encounter yield positive outcomes.

CHAPTER EIGHT

LEADING-EDGE ORGANIZATIONAL SKILLS

The genius (so-called) is only that one who discerns the pattern of things within the confusion of details a little sooner than the average person.

—BEN SHAHN

As I've noted elsewhere in this book, the executive assistant's job is one in which interruptions must be accepted as a constant, unchangeable aspect of the working day. There are always phone calls to handle, crises to resolve, and urgent messages to relay. Of course, this is not to say that the effective executive assistant brings no organizational skills to the table! In this chapter we'll take a brief look at some of the most important steps you can take to tame the chaos.

THE RIGHT FILING SYSTEM FOR YOU (THERE ARE REALLY THREE OF THEM)

You may coordinate documents through printed hard copies, via an impeccably managed (and impeccably backed up) series of files and notations in your computer system, or through an intriguing hybrid of the two. But much of your job will turn on your ability to file and retrieve important documents. There are three basic filing systems your office must incorporate, and that means there are three systems for *you* to implement. Yes, your boss probably has her own computer, but you may rest assured that the job of coordinating the hundreds of files accumulating on her hard disk will eventually fall to you.

Here are the three systems with which you'll need to be familiar.

THE TICKLER FILE

Also called a *pending* file or a *follow-up* file, this group of documents and reminders, sequenced by date, alerts your boss (and you) to particular events that must be attended to in a timely fashion. My favorite is the folder with 12 main compartments, one for each month, and with subfolders for each date of the month. At the beginning of the day, you check the appropriate subfolder for notes on what meetings to schedule, reports to circulate, or thank-you notes to send. (Beware of misfiled entries arising from weekend dates! The payroll staff may need to get new employee information on the first day of January, but if that day falls on a Sunday, you'll need to be sure the tickler goes into the "January 2" slot, or whatever the appropriate date is.)

THE CHRONOLOGICAL FILE

This is a collection of your office's outgoing correspondence, arranged by date and with helpful summaries of subject matter. Some people make the mistake of trying to use their word processing system for this filing chore—without giving any indication of the date of a document's composition in the name of the file. ("Let's see—is LEASE1A.DOC the letter from September, or was that LEASE2C.DOC?") I prefer to get my hands on hard copies of everything, but if you do decide to go the computerized route here, bear in mind that you must find some way to make your document date-specific at a glance.

THE ALPHABETICAL FILE

This is an alphabetically arranged collection of the same correspondence contained in the chronological file. Use the last name of the recipient—or, if it makes more sense to you, the name of the recipient's organization. Your own logical system, consistently applied, is the best one to employ. By the way, your manager's alphabetical file is probably where you'll want to store copies of *incoming* correspondence as well, although your organization may have a different system for you to follow.

These three systems are the ones you'll rely on most to perform one of your most important responsibilities: retrieving documents when your boss needs them. Don't get creative when it comes to storing important documents! Keep it simple. Keep it consistent. And keep it current. Filing systems have a way of collapsing into confusion when you stop attending to them on a daily basis. Because filing is often perceived as among the least enjoyable tasks in the office, it's one that can easily be put aside. It often becomes much *less* enjoyable as a result!

Some words are in order here on the never-to-be-ignored topic of backing up your computer files. My personal preference, as I've already indicated, is to have both hard copies and computer records of important correspondence and vital job materials. I suggest that you follow this approach as well, but I urge you not to consider your hard copies to represent adequate backups of your computerized data. Not only will you want to avoid reentering several weeks' work if something awful happens to your disks, you may also have a very difficult time determining exactly what constitutes the most recent version of a file. Who has time for an archaeological expedition through four different versions of spreadsheet printouts?

Make copies of all your disks (or use your organization's backup technology), and you won't have to redo your work. Remember that work is not backed up until two copies have been made: one for the job site and one for another secure location. Sound contingency planning means early planning; if the sprinkler system goes off for no apparent reason and drenches everything in sight, you'll want to have a dry set of disks or tapes. I suggest a monthly backup of this remote site material.

Backing up your work in the way I've described may *seem* like a terrific waste of time as you're plodding through the various steps required, but sound backup habits are probably among the very *best* investments of your working hours. The truth is that in today's office environment no one has another month to redo a complex project (or series of projects). Like it or not, we live in an era in which that much work—or far more—really does exist in the form of a series of zeros and ones on a computer disk. Strange things have happened to computer disks.

THE TELEPHONE AND ITS MANY CHALLENGES: MAKING SENSE OF THE SEA OF CALLS

Honesty time: Executives resent the amount of time they have to spend on the phone, and in a good many cases that means the executive assistant's primary duty is to field the barrage of telephone calls targeted toward the boss.

Not infrequently you will have to be rather direct about your status as the person who handles your boss's calls. ("I'm sorry, because of the demands on his time, Mr. Big has instructed me to get the name, affiliation, and purpose of the call.") In some other situations you will have to run interference for your boss, and volunteer to help when his schedule is impossible. In still others, you will have to offer the best available summaries of information your boss has not had the opportunity to pass along to important contacts. There are probably 100 different ways for the telephone to intrude on your day, and they are all, more or less by their nature, completely unpredictable. Although the telephone company may be able to supply us with "caller ID" technology, it has yet to grant us "purpose ID" readouts that will let us know which callers want what, and when!

Telephone work represents an extraordinarily important responsibility for the executive assistant. Some people get overwhelmed by the task of coordinating all the calls. For my part, I believe in maintaining scrupulous phone etiquette as a matter of self-preservation.

I'm compulsive when it comes to people's telephone skills. I have very little patience with people who display poor phone manners when they don't get through, or who try to use dishonest means to get through to employees within an organization. That said, I know that not everyone takes the same attitude toward telephone communications, and I like to think that I keep an open mind when it comes to dealing with a wide variety of people over the phone. I have a theory, though: I believe that *one person's* impeccable phone etiquette can have a dramatic impact on the call in question for *both people*. By "outpoliting" the other person, the executive assistant can minimize:

- The number of dead-end sales calls that leave both parties going around in circles
- The frequency and seriousness of crossed conversational wires when dealing with outsiders
- The likelihood that your boss will miss out on something important with regard to calls from people within the organization

I've found that, when you're unfailingly polite, it rubs off on the other person. Fewer calls turn into showdowns. Fewer calls result in long-winded diatribes or sales pitches. Fewer calls conclude in frustration for the other person or you, for that matter. Here, then, are my four suggestions for maintaining an unfailingly polite phone persona, one that will help you get on the right side of your conversation with the caller.

- Don't shoot down salespeople as a matter of course. I say this for three reasons: First, it's rude to dismiss someone instantly. Second, there is a genuine possibility that your boss may be able to benefit from what the salesperson has to offer. Third, a small but vocal percentage of cold callers are under instructions to engage in the highly unprofessional tactic of overwhelming the organization with calls in an effort to get around an executive assistant who's just trying to do her job. In my experience, there are two types of telephone salespeople: those who realize that an executive assistant deserves to be treated with something akin to the same respect as her boss, and those who don't. The beauty of showing unfailing politeness—at least at first—to all phone salespeople is that you can sometimes turn a salesperson from the second category into a salesperson from the first category. So be pleasant, upbeat, and open-minded. Do not react angrily if your caller orders you about, demanding to be put in touch with your boss. Whenever possible, ask an intelligent question about what the person has to offer. Salespeople believe, quite rightly, that the more questions the person on the other end asks, the better the sales call is going. If there doesn't seem to be a good match, say so. If there does, check with your boss, or refer the person to another representative of the company. If you go to the trouble of asking a serious question of the salesperson and you still find the conversation polarized and combative, ask the caller to put the request in writing and thank the person for calling.

Following the procedure I've just outlined usually takes *less* time than trying to dismiss a determined salesperson, and it will dramatically minimize the number of irritating follow-up calls you and others in the organization are likely to receive from the salesperson in question. The bottom line is this: When you ask a question, your no has a better chance of sticking.

- Never sigh into the telephone as you answer it or continue a conversation with someone else in the office when you pick up the line. These are distressingly common problems. Don't let them become yours. The first impression you leave is one of someone who would rather be doing almost *anything* than dealing with the caller. That's a risky undertaking when you don't know who's calling! Similarly, you shouldn't start talking on the telephone until you've completed doing anything that has a prior demand on your attention: sighing, talking with another individual, eating, sneezing, coughing, or anything else.
- Be sure your phone voice is as pleasant and as varied in tone as your normal office voice. An executive assistant who routinely employs a harsh or monotonous phone manner will be doing her manager and herself a disservice. See the advice in Chapter 5 on improving your vocal delivery for some ideas that you can incorporate here.
- Even when things are hectic, make an effort to let the caller know that you truly care about the reason he or she is calling, *whether or not you feel the caller is someone your boss*

would be likely to consider important. In reality, every caller is significant and should be treated with respect.

Not long ago a writer friend of mine told me a story about grace under fire that's worth repeating here. He was at an airport, preparing to board a flight at the end of a long business trip, when an announcement came over the loudspeaker. Because of a faulty landing, a plane had gotten lodged in the mud near the end of a runway. No one was hurt, but the airport was "temporarily shut down," and "significant delays" were expected. While he was waiting in a very long line to try to get more information about the status of his flight, my friend noticed a woman working at her station at one airline's besieged customer service desk. Each and every customer she dealt with was furious. And each and every time she dealt with a new customer, she brought the same unflappably pleasant attitude to her new acquaintance. Such a display of unfailing poise and optimism kept up for well over an hour—the entire time my friend spent in line. If the woman's attitude was turning sour as a result of all the people who were yelling at her, it certainly didn't show. It is possible to maintain poise and an open mind, even in the most chaotic situations, as this woman proved. If her airline job ever falls through, she might want to consider becoming an executive assistant. My guess is that she'd have superb telephone technique.

A WORD OR TWO ABOUT E-MAIL SYSTEMS

One of the most exciting new developments in office communication has been the rise of e-mail. Just as the executive assistant is responsible for handling phone traffic, she is also likely to be her boss's first choice when it comes to sorting through the dense thicket of electronic messages awaiting the boss's reply. The etiquette for e-mail messages is somewhat different from that for other messages, primarily because people seem to write more, and perhaps more carelessly, on computers than they do when sitting in front of a typewriter. A few pointers on dealing with this exciting technology follow.

Just as you would sort through all the telephone messages awaiting your boss's attention, so you must do a quick buzz of all the e-mail updates that think they're going to get a look from the boss. These days, a good many organizations pass along extremely important updates via the electronic mail system. Don't make the mistake of thinking that these messages can wait for a couple of days before they hook up with a pair of human eyes. It's easier to put this task off than you might think; at least a telephone *rings* when someone's trying to reach you. That means a frustrated telemarketer may distract you from an important electronic memo zapped to your manager. Apparently in response to this problem, a good many e-mail systems now feature chimes that go off to alert the recipient of a message's arrival. If yours doesn't do this—actually, even if it does—you must be ever vigilant about wading through the system at least a couple of times a day.

Learn the subtleties of your system's "send" feature inside and out—even if (*especially* if) your boss can't be bothered to. One of the hazards of modern electronic mail is that it can sometimes result in the accidental distribution of sensitive or confidential internal correspondence. Many people take the precaution of designating anything of a potentially inflammatory nature—salary reviews, say, or updates of pending legal problems—*off-limits* to the company's "quick mail" system. This is a sensible enough approach, but it deserves to be combined with a working knowledge of when and how a message is distributed widely. If your boss never quite catches up with the technology in this area—and there's a good chance a busy executive won't—you may want to volunteer to be the one who sends outgoing messages.

OVERUSE OF CAPITAL LETTERS IS THE CYBERWORLD'S EQUIVALENT OF SHOUTING IN THE OTHER PERSON'S EAR. DON'T COMPOSE ALL YOUR MESSAGES WITH THE "CAPS LOCK" KEY STUCK IN THE "ON" POSITION. There. See how much of a difference that makes?

For some reason—probably the increased fluency and

immediacy that accompanies the composition and review of electronic mail—it seems to be *much, much easier to offend people* via electronic mail than it is through a typed memo. Be careful what you and your manager say; many an electronic "joke" has had the unintended effect of starting a battle of electronic memos. The cyberregion's answer to this problem has been the ubiquitous "smiley" character—usually :) or one of its innumerable variations—which alerts the reader to the intended emotion of the typist.

Finally bear in mind that people tend not to read long e-mail messages unless they absolutely have to. When in doubt, keep it as brief as possible.

ORGANIZING THE EXECUTIVE'S TRAVEL

If you like to check details twice, maintain control over things, and display all the foresight necessary to keep disasters from happening—and remember, these are required traits in the successful executive assistant—you will sooner or later learn that your boss's travel plans are your biggest enemy. Why?

Because everything that can go wrong during a road trip usually does. You will probably have become used to the idea that any logistical dilemma is your responsibility. Travel adds the fascinating complication that you must not only solve everything, but also solve everything *hundreds of miles and several time zones away.* For most executive assistants this game of "where is he now, when is he calling back, how is he going to get what he needs" and "what can go wrong next" makes each day of the road trip an exciting adventure. There are a number of things you may be while your boss is on the road—uncertain, overwrought, exhausted, reliant to an uncomfortable degree on incompetent servicepeople—but it's a pretty safe bet that you won't be bored.

Here are nine ideas that, to paraphrase an old prayer, will help you plan for what you can plan for, deal with what you can't, and encourage the wisdom to distinguish between the two while your boss is out of the office.

- Start early. The bigger the head start you get on the task of arranging all the wheres and whens of your boss's trip, the less likely you are to have to deal with some last-minute oversight. There is an inherent problem with the "start early" school of thought, however. In order to get an early start, you must know when your boss plans to leave and return and with whom she will be traveling. That means, by definition, that *your boss* must know these things, and you may have to engage in some not-so-subtle lobbying to bring about finalization on these key points. One technique known to do the trick: a brief memo outlining the available options, with check boxes by each possibility and a subtle reminder of the looming deadline for purchasing tickets (with the attendant fare differential if the decision is put off). A good many bosses will check a box and hand the memo back to you.
- Assume that the travel people with whom you're working don't always have current information; they *certainly* don't have all the alternatives. This may seem like an overly cynical outlook, but trust me, it is borne out by years of hard-won experience. Even if you do manage to hook up with a superior travel agent, and you should certainly try, you simply cannot trust that this person will get everything right. And if that's true of a travel agent with whom you have worked hard to develop a solid professional relationship, you can imagine what sometimes happens one or two steps down the line, when harried airline workers or hotel staff members get into the act. Call the airlines and reconfirm the price, date, time, and attendant ground-travel arrangements for every flight ticket you hold in your hand. Call and reconfirm the price, reservation number, service specifications, and applicable dates of every hotel at which your boss is planning to stay. Mark my words: Before you've been at the job for too long, you will find something horrific waiting to happen. Which brings me to the next item…
- Build plenty of extra time into the schedule. As anyone who's spent any time dealing with commercial airlines can attest, these organizations don't always run like clockwork. Flights are delayed. Flights get canceled. Flights fall victim to surre-

alistically disorganized airline executives. I have heard tell from a reliable source of a certain major airline that attempted, for some time, to route *nine flights* through a single gate, all (theoretically) leaving within the same 1-hour period. This may seem like the type of blissfully ignorant mismanagement of resources that might endure for a day or two. But the sad fact is that the airline went on with this hectic arrangement for months—even though some flights were *always* delayed as a result and even though huge throngs of angry customers gathering dutifully about their assigned gate *always* ended up being confused and significantly inconvenienced. This type of incompetence is, alas, all too common, and it's a better-than-even bet that your boss is going to encounter it at some point during an extended trip. The question is: Will your boss have a schedule that's generous enough to accommodate such problems? Will she be able to make it to the hotel desk, bedraggled but *there,* before midnight? Or is a long nap in the terminal and a missed morning meeting in the cards? Granted, you will not always have the luxury of being able to insert an extra "safety hour" (at least) into your boss's schedule. But you should certainly try to do so whenever the opportunity arises.

- Obtain tickets and boarding passes in advance. Make sure the seat assignment meets your executive's preference. The less your boss has to worry about once he makes it to the airport, the better. For long trips that require multiple stops, prepare a multiple-envelope packet with each set of tickets and boarding passes—and car rental information, if that's necessary—in easy-to-find compartments. The idea is to let your boss push the arrival time to the airport as late as is necessary; if a meeting gobbles up an extra half hour of your boss's day, you want him to be able to drop off a rental car, sprint to the departure gate, pull out a clearly marked envelope, and make it on the plane a minute or so before takeoff.
- Choose the hotel according to the executive's specifications *and* the communications facilities that will be available to you when it's time to get in touch with the boss. Sometimes man-

agers focus more on style than on practicality. Of course, you must make sure that the hotel has all the ambiance and service amenities your boss needs; make sure, too, that it offers the incoming and outgoing fax capability, phone service with voicemail functions, and computerized data access for laptop use that your manager will require. Make sure your manager has all the information necessary to access these facilities.

- Don't forget to confirm and reconfirm all the surface connections and directions, too! If your boss will be using a rental car in an unfamiliar city, you will need to find out where the car may be picked up and dropped off. Make sure maps are provided. You will also need to develop comprehensible directions informing your manager of how to get from point A to point B. This may seem to be a simple enough task—just call the hotel and ask for a series of instructions—but even conscientiously recited and transcribed directions can be the cause of endless headaches on the road. The reason? People who give directions are usually familiar with the city in question, but *unfamiliar* with the particular hazards faced by a newcomer. It's not uncommon for a "local" to advise someone to "take a left on Broad Street"—but forget that the intersection at which the driver is supposed to turn does not boast a sign *identifying* Broad Street! These potential problems, and a dozen or so just as intimidating, can make surface travel a relentless nightmare from which your boss (and, by extension, you) will have great difficulty recovering. Get the directions from an unimpeachable source (I recommend the American Automobile Association), and confirm them by means of a discussion with a knowledgeable insider who can point you toward *landmarks* as well as street names. This advice is particularly important for travelers to such cities as Atlanta (where every third street is named Peachtree, just to confuse visiting Northerners) and Boston (where the notion of consistently identifying *any* street with a legible sign is apparently considered a slur against the intuitive skills of local drivers).
- Once you've arranged everything, commit all the details to a clear, easy-to-read itinerary, a duplicate master document that

you and your boss can both consult—and make sense of—at a moment's notice. Be sure to include primary and fax telephone numbers for all the hotels where your boss will be staying.

- Be prepared for a little—all right, a lot of—extra library and telephone work if your boss plans to travel abroad. The problems increase in number and complexity when your boss decides to travel to a foreign country, but in most cases the amount of time at your disposal stays the same. Among the issues to consider: Should you arrange for a translator and/or an escort? (Making sense of directions in an unfamiliar American city is one thing; doing so in Tokyo or St. Petersburg is quite another.) Do you need to arrange for a particular off-hour time for telephone contact? ("Near the end of the day" may work if you're in New York and your boss is in Chicago, but a 9-hour time difference may put more of a crimp in things. You may have to arrange for base touching to be done in the early morning or late evening via your home phone.) Are all the necessary passports and visas in order? (Another bit of detail work that falls into the "get a head start" category.) Does your boss have all the necessary local currency he will need for the trip? (This, too, will require some planning. As a fallback, your boss should be informed about the most convenient place and method for converting American cash to local currency while on the road, in case an emergency arises that a credit card transaction won't accommodate.) What are the prices like? What are the weather conditions likely to be in the near future? Develop a contact who will be able to assist your manager in these areas.

It is appropriate to mention here the "Manual of Desk Practices", which is a valuable resource to you, your executive, and to anyone who substitutes for you. This up-to-date manual, which is on disk and in hard copy, records the pertinent data (use discretion on sensitive, private information) on how to handle the key aspects of your position. It should contain lists of key callers, personal and business contacts; explain how mail is sorted and distributed; outline the style in which messages are delivered; detail how meetings are arranged; list all key personnel, both in terms of department and areas of responsibility. This manual should also detail traveling needs (such as restaurants frequented, aircraft and seating preferences, special dietary needs). Whatever practices support the needs of your office and enhances your efficiency is to be included in this manual.

- Finally, expect the unexpected. No matter how many contingency plans you set up, no matter how many corners you look around, *something* you hadn't counted on will happen while your boss is on the road. The question is, will it fluster you and throw you off your game, or will you be able to summon your best, most inspired response to the situation and engage in some creative long-distance problem solving?

CHAPTER NINE

THE COMPANY SPOKESPERSON—MASTERING CUSTOMER SERVICE AND PUBLIC RELATIONS TASKS

Always do right. This will gratify some people and astonish the rest.

—Mark Twain

In today's office you must sometimes act not only as your boss's representative, but as a spokesperson for the entire organization. Why? Usually because your boss is overbooked. World-class executive assistants are able to help cultivate relationships; they are trusted to assist in the work of the executive.

The idea is to handle the overflow for your boss as gracefully as possible when it comes to situations that require communication with the various people who *don't* work for your organization, but who *do* have the ability to make life difficult for your boss. Herewith some ideas for interacting with outsiders with precision, poise, and clear thinking.

HANDLING ANGRY OR ABUSIVE CUSTOMERS EFFECTIVELY

It's a fact of contemporary business life: Today's companies are trying to get closer and closer to the customer through quality service, and a good many of them are making the ability to deal politely, directly, and capably with customer concerns a central part of their formal mission statement. At many organizations, this means, in effect, that employees in the company are, or should consider themselves to be, part of the "customer service department" in some respect.

Dealing with customers—especially *testy* customers—is a fine art, one that no one should expect to master overnight. Given the healthy emphasis on customer focus in so many of today's companies, solid customer service is an art that is worth refining and polishing over time for any worker who supports an executive. The four principles laid out below aren't the last word on handling questions and complaints from the people who use what your company makes or benefit from what your company does, but they'll certainly get you pointed in the right direction.

Rule 1: Find a Way to Say, "You've Come to the Right Place." Customers, testy or otherwise, want to hear that they've made it through the maze of the organization's structure to reach an Honest to Goodness Human Being Who'll Help Them Resolve the Question at Hand. It may be tempting to transfer a call to the "department that handles X," but ask yourself: How do you feel when someone does that to you? Do you look forward to retelling your story to the second (or the third, or the fourth, or the fifth) person in a row? Customer service guru Michael Ramundo advocates "ownership" of a customer call or contact—which means either committing to resolving the problem on your own or assuming responsibility for explaining it capably to the next person down the line, and informing the customer of the response status at all times. It's a great idea, and it's one that is far more likely to earn you the respect and goodwill of that feisty caller.

Rule 2: Admit There Was a Problem if There Really Was One. Various organizations take different positions on this one; some feel that it's legally too risky to admit fault or blame in a complaint situation unless the particulars have been thoroughly reviewed by several layers of management. If that's a company policy, then you must adhere to it, but I couldn't disagree more with the approach, and there are a good many successful companies who feel exactly the way I do. In addition to wanting to hook up with someone who will do something other than transfer the call, the customer wants to talk to someone who will say the company made a mistake when that is clearly the case. Yes, a certain amount of common sense is necessary to make this principle work, but what's new about that? The reality is that it is generally the persistently infuriated customers who decide to take legal recourse, and the single best way to keep people from being infuriated is to talk to them patiently and intelligently for 1 or 2 minutes at a stretch (see Rule 1 above). Whenever possible, acknowledge oversights without sounding like you're dodging the issue. If there was a problem, apologize on behalf of the organization. It makes a difference to secure help for the caller, and to follow up to make sure the problem has been resolved. Doing so helps transform rage into goodwill and effective customer relations.

Rule 3: Let the Person Blow Off a Little Steam. Some customers are determined to yell. Some are bound to upset someone else's day as badly as their own has been upset. Some are bound and determined to use aggressive language. *Very few* customers, however, will persist in these tactics indefinitely. Let the person rant for a moment, then…

Rule 4: Humanize the Exchange. The fourth weapon in your arsenal: treating the customer as a fellow person. This delivers magnificent results. The best approach is to empathize with the customer's predicament, using phrases like the following, delivered with genuine concern: "I know just how you must feel; I'm a mother myself." "That must have been frustrating to have had so little advance notice about the schedule change." "Well, it sounds like having to return for repairs all over again must have been very inconvenient. And I'll bet it didn't win you any points with your manager to have to bring your computer in for service and miss a day of work." By showing that you're not a heartless bureaucrat, that you're someone who understands what it's like to deal with unexpected problems, you will almost certainly win points with the customer.

Trust me: If you follow Rules 1, 2, 3, and 4, you will soon become a master at resolving the vast majority of problem calls and visits.

DEALING WITH THE MEDIA

Handling the press is an art, especially considering the tendency of some reporters to launch attack pieces while pretending to do research for a story that will be flattering. Under what circumstances does an executive assistant respond to the press? Here are five basic strategies for dealing with the press that will help you act in the best interests of your manager and your organization.

Strategy 1: Discuss all Unsolicited Press Queries with Your Manager Before You Respond. Your manager may have access to important information that you don't. This is one situation in which it is much better to err on the side of caution than to act on your own instincts. Even if the reporter sounds enthusiastic, open-minded, and eager to pursue your organization's side of the story, you are best advised *not* to open up with a reporter who contacts you without clearing the response with your boss. (Responses to your organization's press packets are, as a rule, a different matter. See Strategies 3 and 4 below.)

Strategy 2: Never Dignify a Negative With Repetition. If your organization *is* under assault from the media, and it has fallen to you to deal with press queries, you must strive, as the politicians put it, "to stay on message." The basic rule is to say nothing you don't want to see in print—even in the form of a denial. This means having a concise, responsible, and compelling account of your organization's perspective on events; it also means not being distracted by questions designed to throw you off guard. In brief, you must decline the invitation to dwell on the other side's charges, and that means not repeating them. Focus on the positives, even when that requires straying from the formal boundaries of the question:

Tough question: "What is your response to allegations that your firm deliberately inserted rubber cement instead of vanilla filling into your chocolate cookies?"

Bad answer: "We never pumped rubber cement into our cookies. It's not true."

Good answer: "It has always been our company's policy to uphold the most stringent safety standards in our plants. We are examining the current claims, and nobody is more interested than Cookieco in finding out exactly what has happened here. When we've completed our thorough internal review of the reports that surfaced, we'll be providing detailed summaries of all our findings."

Strategy 3: Think of the Reporter's Audience. Has your boss asked you to draft a press release? One of the most common complaints people in the media have is that those who seek their attention forget that reporters have a job to do, too. Their job is to win the interest and, not infrequently, overcome the short attention spans of a large audience. It may be top-of-the list news for you and your boss that your company has decided, at long last, to launch a new product ("Marriss Computer Announces New Data Retrieval Service with Real Estate Application"), but is the decision itself really something that's likely to capture the interest of a large number of readers and viewers? Most press releases detail stories that don't address the interests of the reporter's audience, and so most reporters (not surprisingly) throw away the vast majority of the press releases they receive. Instead of focusing on your company's decisions or steps, why not take a good, long look at the publication or broadcast that is most typical of the type you're trying to reach—and develop several drafts of your press release with an eye toward matching the style and interest level of the stories that you see? Emphasize the unusual, the beneficial, the dangerous, the trendy—in short, anything that will help you convince a reporter that you're just as interested in getting a reader or viewer to stop short and pay attention as the reporter is. ("Now Homebuyers Can Do Their Househunting over the Internet!") Don't be surprised if this means downplaying (but not eliminating) your company's name—and don't be surprised if you end up writing something that runs more or less "as is" in the media outlet to which you send it. (Reporters are just as busy as the rest of us—busier, usually—and one of the very best ways to win media attention is to write the story "to fit" so that members of the media have to do little or nothing to work it into shape.)

Strategy 4: When Trying to Win Attention from the Press, Develop an "Expandable" Message. In other words, become intimately familiar with a number of variations on your press release. There should be short (one-sentence) versions you can use to win initial interest during phone conversations with members of the media, 30-second versions you or someone in your organization can use to fill sound bytes, 5-minute versions you or someone in your organization can display during longer interviews, and full-length versions for reporters who want to do extended feature pieces. If your boss is likely to be the person who deals with the media, it is a good idea for you to develop written "talking points" that outline varying-length versions of the same message for review before (or, discreetly, during) interviews.

Strategy 5: When Trying to Win Attention from the Press, Use the Quickest, Most Cost-Effective Method Imaginable. Ready for a surprise? Your 100-piece mailing may be, comparatively speaking, a waste of time and money. We've already seen that the vast majority of mailed press queries received by reporters get tossed into the garbage can without a thought. These people have schedules that are just as tight as yours, and if they don't see an *immediate* match with their needs, they will not read your material, no matter how painstaking its preparation. (And by the way, if you mail the press kit to the *organization*, rather than to a particular reporter, you're almost certainly wasting the postage.) So why not call first? It may take you some time to track down the person most likely to deal with the topic to which you're trying to draw attention, but it will be time well spent. What's more, you'll be able to *customize* the press kit you send to the needs of the media outlet and thereby increase the likelihood of your organization's receiving coverage. Track down (and confirm) information in media directories—you can find these in your local library. Then use the one-sentence summary discussed in Strategy 4 above as the basis for a polite, upbeat phone call with a reporter. That conversation could sound something like this:

YOU: Hello, is this Mr. Bill Watson?

REPORTER: Yes, this is he.

YOU: Hello, Bill! This is Helen Kite at Marriss Computer; thanks a lot for taking my call. You handle high-tech stories for the *Globe,* as I understand it?

REPORTER: That's right—but it's kind of busy around here right now...

YOU: I understand completely, that's why I'll make this quick. We have a new piece of software that allows home buyers to review photographs and descriptions of real estate property via our nationwide database. It's accessible through the Internet. A lot of people are calling it a very exciting advance in technology, and I wanted to know if this was the type of story you deal with.

REPORTER: Could be. Through the Internet, huh? Do people have to pay for the software, or for access to the database?

YOU: They pay once for the software; we maintain the database, and customers have unlimited free access to the database. Would you like to see a press kit?

REPORTER: Yeah, I'll tell you what. Why don't you send me one, and send one along to Fred Hanbury, too—he does our real-estate reporting. He might be interested in this as well, but he'd probably be more likely to approach it from the consumer's point of view than I would. I'd be more likely to take a look at the technology. If you can send a copy of the software, I'd love to give it a test drive.

You can uncover more leads for placement of your story with a call like this than you can with a blind mailing, and you can highlight particular aspects of the story for individual reporters. What if the person you talk to doesn't want to see your press kit? Well, you can always ask about (and note for future use) what kinds of stories that person does have an interest in pursuing. Even if you reach a complete dead end, you've saved the time and energy associated with printing, mailing, and following up on a press kit that wasn't going to be read anyway!

TIPS FOR BETTER LISTENING (YOUR SECRET WEAPON IN DEALING WITH OUTSIDERS)

Your strategy for dealing with outsiders as a representative of your company is a fairly simple two-step affair: listen first, and talk second. Whether you're dealing with a reporter, a customer, or some other important category of nonemployee, you are much likelier to be able to resolve the situation and get your boss's message across if you listen for the other person's key objectives, and then work to find a way to get your own ideas across in a nonconfrontational way. Here are some suggestions that will help you build a positive image for your organization by means of enhanced listening skills.

If it's at all possible, let your conversational partner know, through your choice of tone and setting, that he or she has your undivided attention. Most of us spend a large chunk of our lives negotiating unsatisfying short-term conflicts over hectic telephone lines, harshly lit customer-service counters, and imposing "reception" desks. One of the best ways to encourage your conversational partner to open up is to make it clear from the outset that you are *willing to make the time to deal with the issue at hand.* (Whether you have time to spare isn't really the issue; the assumption is that you're dealing with someone whom your boss wants to keep happy and that means you *must* send this message.) If conducting your conversation by telephone is unavoidable, make it clear to the person on the other end of the line that this conversation is the only one you'll be doing, that ending it quickly is not your primary objective, and that you hope to get a full understanding of the situation as the other person sees it.

Two brief observations on the topic of getting people to open up on the telephone. First, your *attitude* and tone of voice are just as important as the words you select; second, you may well find that calls you approach in this way conclude *sooner* than ones in which you and the caller fight for control of the conversation. If you are holding a face-to-face meeting, make every effort to conduct the conversation in a conference room or other quiet place where your guest can take a seat, and don't keep the individual waiting in the lobby if you can possibly avoid doing so. Physical setting, and the sense of being attended to that we all desire in dealing with others, will have a major impact on whether your conversational partner decides to take an antagonistic approach. Do your level best to keep delays and distractions to a minimum. *Full attention* is what your conversational partner is after.

During the "small talk" period of a meeting, make a point of asking appropriate questions about the other person's background, family, and interests. Many of today's companies boast a get-right-to-the-point work culture, which is fine for employees but may be just a bit intimidating to visitors. If this is the case in your organization, make the effort to alter your greeting style, and perhaps compensate for your boss's or someone else's brusqueness, for your guest's benefit. If you simply shake hands and demand to "cut to the chase," you will run the risk of alienating some of your contacts.

Insofar as possible, stay away from the rule book when discussing your conversational partner's objective. It may be tempting to cite company policy to customers, reporters, or others, but when you do so you run the risk of changing the dynamic of the interaction for the worse. (Which would you rather deal with, a person or a bureaucracy?) If you must deal with an organizational hurdle, make an effort to present it as a *shared* challenge—one that you and your conversational partner face together—and remember that you should *never* interrupt the other person to inform him or her that something "can't be done." Even if it can't, you're better off letting your partner finish outlining the problem and then demonstrating your desire to find some way to make the system work in this situation.

As much as you can, note the other person's terminology—and use that phrasing, not the organization's, in dealing with the situation. Make an effort to stay away from technical phrases or in-house jargon when working with outsiders. Language is a powerful, and often intimidating, factor in human relationships, and a great deal depends on whose "code words" are adopted in addressing a problem or opportunity. Many a frazzled customer has been instantly calmed by the sensitive replaying of key words and phrases. ("Mr. Howard, if getting your office back up and running is what you want, then getting your office back up and running is what we're going to do.") Often, the sheer joy of having escaped organization-speak will make all the difference; you may be surprised at how much this seemingly modest step can accomplish when it comes to establishing or reestablishing a good connection with an outsider. If you can find an appropriate opportunity to employ the outsider's terminology during your interaction, do so—but remember that this is *not* the same thing as letting someone put words into your mouth!

CHAPTER TEN

PERSONAL, PROFESSIONAL, AND SPIRITUAL DEVELOPMENT

Our greatest need is for a spiritual improvement in ourselves and in our relations with our fellow human beings, but this is a need that science and technology in themselves cannot meet.

—ARNOLD J. TOYNBEE

There is little use denying that the executive assistant's job can be a stressful one, and still less in imagining that the many technological challenges that are part and parcel of her workday always result in a smoother, more serene outlook on the world. In a job such as this one, when poise and balance in the face of crisis are of paramount importance, an ongoing commitment to personal growth and stress management is perhaps the most important unwritten element of the job description. You can't progress in your career—or in your life, for that matter—if your job overwhelms your sense of identity. A successful executive assistant knows how to nurture and replenish her most important asset: herself.

For me, this commitment to ongoing renewal carries a spiritual component. I realize that by focusing on spirituality as an aspect of stress management and personal development, I run the risk of alienating some people. Yet the idea of an illuminating, unifying, all-inclusive purpose and the notion of a greater destiny underlying one's work and personal life are so important to me in my own ongoing efforts at self-renewal that I want to share them with you here. If you feel more comfortable substituting another approach in implementing the ideas that follow, please feel free to do so!

FIVE IDEAS FOR STRENGTHENING YOUR ON-THE-JOB COMPOSURE

Here are some techniques that may help you become more resilient in your ability to face, in a centered way, the many challenges and obstacles likely to present themselves during your working day. The first idea (which I recommend highly) will initially take up only 10 minutes or so of your morning; the rest can be incorporated in less than a minute or two during the day, as required.

- Take some time for meditation. Before you begin your day, find a quiet, comfortable place to sit; no, crossed legs aren't necessary. Keep your eyes half-closed, and directed toward the floor. Count your deep in and out breaths for 10 minutes. You may want to use an alarm clock to monitor the time. Now, then: What are you trying to accomplish? Nothing. The idea is to follow your own breath in and out and slowly let your mind empty itself of its stockpiled commentary, observation, and analysis. When a thought interrupts your counting, don't criticize yourself, or think about how poor a meditator you are. Head back to the number 1 and start again. When you're done, you'll probably be feeling more grounded, more serene, more in control of yourself. Keep it up! Work your 10-minute stretch into your everyday routine. Feeling ambitious? Try for 12 minutes tomorrow, then 14, then 16...The first time around is the toughest. After a while, you'll be up to a half hour alone with yourself and your breath every day. You'll be a happier, more integrated person if you follow this routine, and you will also be much likelier to enjoy your job (among other things).
- Breathe deeply from your diaphragm when you feel the effects of stress. Some people choose to take the breath as an opportunity to recall a silent personal mantra (or a brief com-

forting phrase such as "almost all the things that aggravate me turn out all right in the end"). Others simply take the opportunity to breathe, which is probably mantra enough. One Buddhist teacher informs her students that the object of life is to imitate the Weebles—you remember, those dolls from the 1970s that wobbled but never fell down—by having a strong enough center to see through nearly any challenge. Breathing deeply, she noted, is an important part of maintaining that center.

- Change your locale. If only for a minute or two, take a break from the setting in which you find stress closing in on you. If there is a particular place you always associate with stressful activity, training yourself to take a brief private moment in a hallway, lobby, or outdoor area can amount to something comparable to a survival skill.
- Bring an apple and an apple peeler to work. When you feel a stressful situation beginning to challenge your center, excuse yourself for just a moment and find someplace where you can quietly set about peeling the apple without distraction. Do it carefully, observantly, for at least a minute. The care you extend in completing this task will help you regain your composure. *Eating* the apple is a good idea, too. Have you ever noticed that stressful moments tend to happen when we're hungry?
- One of the most important common tenets of the great religions of the world is the idea that women and men must learn to reject fear and accept its opposite, love. (You probably thought *hate* was the opposite of love, didn't you? As it turns out, it's fear.) When your own limitations stare you in the face, the best way to react is with self-acceptance and a commitment to banish the paralyzing effects of fear and insecurity. The most effective way I know of to do this is to take a moment to listen to a piece of music that is confident, not fearful. Music is very powerful stuff; for most of us, it's instant emotional reinforcement. You will probably have your own nominees for musical selections that help you banish fear; my own tastes run to opera and classical music. Others I know like to listen to the bells and gongs

and chantings of Tibetan monks. Whatever music banishes fear for you, use it.

CHANNELING YOUR EMOTIONS POSITIVELY

A word of warning: Some of the emotions that you may feel during your day-to-day work as an executive assistant may be quite strong. *Simply opting not to express them is not a solution.*

Whether you decide to employ one of the stress reduction ideas discussed above, to embark on a doctor-supervised exercise program (a good idea in and of itself), to attend a stress management workshop, or to pursue all these options, odds are you will have to do *something* to deal with the stress associated with your job. Don't bottle it all up—you may just explode someday! A healthy diet and a consistent exercise program are a must.

Let's remember: The job in question is one in which you are responsible for just about anything that goes wrong in your executive's daily work life. Strictly speaking, it's a job that's impossible to get right—and that means any attempt to expect total perfection from yourself (or others) is likely to end in disappointment.

Don't fight the emotions you feel. Let them tell you what you should do in response to the many demands of your difficult job. The next step could be a racquetball game, or it could be a meditation retreat. Whatever it is, listen to your own internal voice. Listen to what your spirit is telling you: Take care of yourself.

The spirit rules. The mind acts. The body follows.

Emotional responses live within the mind, where the ego gets to play out its many dances. In trying times, I remind myself that everything moves, that the people with whom I'm upset today will be the people who are partnering with me tomorrow. Emotions are transient. They are also potentially lethal if you allow them to take over any number of situations you will face as an executive assistant. Appealing to spiritual resources—the summoning forces—will help you deal pragmatically and responsibly with the emotions you feel. Appealing to spiritual resources will help you step back and gain a sense of detachment. Daily, I endeavor to meet the challenge to acquire the maturity to look at what I believe from many different perspectives and to see how those beliefs affect my life.

It has been my experience that as an emotionally detached observer, I make a better manager of my life, my work, and the people with whom I must interact daily. Achieving a sense of detachment helps me deal with emotions as internal responses that must be attended to, rather than as the correct response to a given external situation.

OF PROFESSIONAL GROWTH

The executive assistant's job, as we've seen, is not a static one. It is at the cutting edge. That's a great place to learn, but it's not the *only* place. After all, you may be good at picking things up on the fly, but you shouldn't be expected to improvise your way through *everything* if you're going to grow and learn to make a more significant contribution.

When people stop growing, they start dying. So keep on growing! If you are working for the right kind of boss, you will be in a good position to ask for, and receive, permission to attend appropriate seminars, workshops, and continuing-education programs. These will benefit not only you, of course, but the organization that employs you. You may have to speak up to win the right to attend these functions, but it is well worth the effort—especially when you take into account that many companies these days have cut their internal training budgets down to zero! Ask your boss about attending programs that will help you improve your skills in the areas where you feel you are in the best position to make a greater contribution. These programs could include computer classes, accounting workshops, human resources management seminars, classes in leadership, management, and supervisory skills, or anything else that represents a sound investment for both you and the organization for which you work.

EPILOGUE: THE ROAD AHEAD

Who forces time is pushed back by time; who yields to time finds time on his side.

—THE TALMUD

That's it—the best advice I have to offer of winning, succeeding in, and thriving in the most challenging, rewarding job I know.

As we close the book, I want to ask you to remember that performance and integrity are important antidotes to the power disease also known as *hubris.* World-class executive assistants combine the mastery of highly specialized technical expertise with the ability to work effectively in teams by forming productive relationships with other people.

I hope this book has helped you gain greater insight into the many opportunities inherent in the packed schedules, endless detail checking, and multiple roles associated with the job of executive assistant. Most of the people with whom I discuss this job come away saying something like: "It's so big—there must never be enough time in the day to get everything done." A select few come away saying something like: "It's so big—it must be really satisfying when you make it to the end of a day!"

Here's hoping you fall into that second category. If you do, you may rest assured that you possess the right outlook for success as an executive assistant.

Good luck!

APPENDIX I

ORGANIZATIONS YOU MAY WISH TO CONTACT

Forty Plus Club of New York
(Offers assistance to job seekers over 40 years of age)
15 Park Row
New York, NY 10038
212/233-6086

National Business Women's Association
9100 Ward Parkway
P.O. Box 8728
Kansas City, MO 64114-0728
913/432-7755

National Federation of Business and Professional Women's Clubs
2012 Massachusetts Avenue
Washington, DC 20036-2990
202/293-1100

Professional Secretaries International
10502 N.W. Ambassador Drive
Kansas City MO 64153
816/891-6600

Women's Education and Industrial Union
356 Boylston Street
Boston MA 02116
617/536-5651

APPENDIX II

FOR THE EXECUTIVE

A BRIEF OVERVIEW OF THE ART OF HIRING THE RIGHT EXECUTIVE ASSISTANT

Finding an executive assistant may well be the most important hire you ever make. Remember that the goal is to find someone who is a good *balance* for your talents and predispositions. This may mean you should fight a (natural!) inclination to hire someone whose outlook mirrors your own in most respects. At the same time, the complementary nature of the executive assistant's role also demands a certain elusive ability to meld one's way of thinking with that of one's boss. You may have to look for a while before you find the person who is different enough from you to complement your own skill set, and similar enough to follow your lead. At the Duncan Group, we believe that personality fit is the single most important factor for a good working relationship. Six key questions can help you find the perfect fit.

- *Have you thought about what your own busiest time of the day is?* Although you will want to hire someone who "fills your gaps" in any number of ways, you probably *won't* want to hook up with someone whose peak productivity period is diametrically opposed to your own. "Morning person" executives do best with "morning person" assistants; "afternoon people" executives do best with "afternoon people" assistants.
- *Have you determined the job's title?* This will have a major impact on the way the applicant perceives the job. As I've

made clear elsewhere in this book, I much prefer "*executive coordinator* to *secretary, assistant,* or *executive assistant.* You may decide that the coordinator title is the one that best reflects your own conception of the job; there are any number of others to consider as well.

- *Have you composed a thorough and realistic written job description?* The job summary should feature not only all the relevant technical and clerical skills—word processing, dictation skills, detail ability, and the like—but also a brief summary of the kind of work you expect this person to perform in coordinating aspects of your personal life (scheduling social events, handling finances and contacts with family, and so on). It's better to specify these parts of the job up front than to hire someone who isn't expecting duties in these areas and who lacks the required skills to be successful.
- *Have you established key skills that will be evaluated by written tests?* In addition to the ubiquitous typing test, you will probably want to test the applicants for their proofreading, grammar, decision-making capacity, ability to organize, attention to detail, and vocabulary skills. (The tests appearing in Appendix 3 of this book cover many of these areas.) If you expect the assistant to compose text for you—and a good many executives do—you will probably want to incorporate some kind of essay test as well.
- *Have you prepared a collection of interview questions to ask?* See Chapter 4 for a list of some of the most popular questions.
- *Have you vowed to "sleep on" the decision before announcing it to your selected candidate?* Before you make a formal offer and begin a (possibly protracted) round of salary negotiations, be sure that the person you offer the job to really is the one who's likely to make your life easier on a day-to-day basis. I recommend at least two face-to-face interviews with the candidate and perhaps a joint visit to a nonwork setting (such as a restaurant) to get an idea of the personal chemistry you two share—or don't. Even after you've checked all appropriate references and feel quite sure you've found the right person, I recommend waiting for 24 hours before you

announce your decision. Once you make the job offer, you must be able to stand behind it with no misgivings. This is not the kind of hire you want to make by relying exclusively on your "gut instinct."

Finally, remember that hiring and retaining the executive assistant means paying people what they're worth and offering the right challenges. People tend to stick around in this job when they're paid fairly, when they enjoy what they do and feel fulfilled by it, and when they get fulfillment from working as part of a winning team.

A BRIEF OVERVIEW OF THE ART OF DELIVERING A PERFORMANCE REVIEW FOR YOUR EXECUTIVE ASSISTANT

There is still a myth among some managers that performance reviews are somehow perfunctory affairs, 5- to 10-minute annual meetings that require little thought or planning. If the person has a problem, you point it out. If the person is doing good work, you say so and outline the raise.

That kind of standard won't fly in today's team-first workplace, and it is certainly unlikely to lead to long-term job satisfaction on the part of your executive assistant. I recommend scheduled *quarterly* performance reviews not tied to compensation, but to development each of at least 30 minutes in duration, regardless of how well or poorly you feel your assistant is performing. If there are areas in which your assistant needs to improve significantly, you should be discussing and monitoring them at least this often. Ask your assistant to write out her job description and her plans for self-development, complete with target dates.

If you've hooked up with a star performer, you should be sure that message gets across, in detail, at least once a quarter, just to be sure your hero feels appreciated and doesn't fly off for parts unknown. For people who fall in between, a quarterly performance review schedule, coordinated with your organization's *annual* salary review process, may make the results of the year-end "raise watch" less of a shock.

During your review session, you must offer specific written and verbal assessments of your assistant's performance in all the areas set out in the formal job description. Emphasize the positive aspects of the assistant's performance first, and be upbeat about the person's aptitudes and contributions. (If the person you're reviewing *has* no bright spots to point to—although this will happen so rarely as to be hardly worth discussing—you may want to talk to your human resources department about the best way to use the review process to establish a paper trail that will protect your company in the event of a termination.) When the time comes to focus on areas for improvement, point out that everyone on the face of the earth, including you, can stand to improve in some area. Then briefly and tactfully outline the *specific, quantifiable* goal you want your assistant to hit by the time you meet again 3 months hence.

If you're feeling particularly brave (and you want to deepen your assistant's trust in you as a person), conclude the meeting by turning the tables! Ask your assistant what areas *you* should improve in to make working together a more harmonious task. Please note that, in the best cases—those in which assistant and executive truly match up well—this type of mutual review is a positive, eye-opening experience for both parties.

VOCABULARY SKILLS TEST

How strong are your vocabulary skills? Take this test to find out. Which of the four options comes closest to the meaning of the italicized word?

Check the answer key at the end of this appendix. If you score correctly on fewer than 42 of the questions, you need to expand and enrich your vocabulary. Head to your local library and check out a book that will help you grow in this area. Read, read, read!

Egregious comes closest to meaning:
a. barren
b. glaring
c. repetitive
d. minor
(The correct answer is *b*.)

1. *Omnipotent* comes closest to meaning:
   a. all-powerful
   b. frustrated
   c. relaxed
   d. attentive
2. *Altruism* comes closest to meaning:
   a. sarcasm
   b. intelligence
   c. generosity
   d. open-mindedness
3. *Stringent* comes closest to meaning:
   a. elaborate
   b. unimaginative
   c. professional
   d. strict

4. *Bemused* comes closest to meaning:
   a. preoccupied
   b. disturbed
   c. confused
   d. uninterested
5. *Infer* comes closest to meaning:
   a. conclude
   b. imply
   c. decide
   d. begin
6. *Capriciously* comes closest to meaning:
   a. joyously
   b. impulsively
   c. predictably
   d. hilariously
7. *Reciprocate* comes closest to meaning:
   a. seek vengeance
   b. act hastily
   c. respond in kind
   d. act as mediator
8. *Intercede* comes closest to meaning:
   a. volunteer
   b. step in
   c. interrogate
   d. undermine
9. *Abrogated* comes closest to meaning:
   a. invalidated
   b. completed
   c. reread
   d. overseen
10. *Specious* comes closest to meaning:
    a. intelligent
    b. misleading
    c. loud
    d. bitter

11. *Stereotypes* comes closest to meaning:
 a. double meanings
 b. predictable descriptions
 c. powerful images
 d. plot twists

12. *Surreptitious* comes closest to meaning:
 a. intolerant
 b. rude
 c. secret
 d. disruptive

13. *Retrospect* comes closest to meaning:
 a. truth
 b. hindsight
 c. fairness
 d. summary

14. *Strident* comes closest to meaning:
 a. detailed
 b. harsh
 c. brief
 d. sentimental

15. *Tenuous* comes closest to meaning:
 a. attentive
 b. logical
 c. weak
 d. dangerous

16. *Excise* comes closest to meaning:
 a. eliminate
 b. proofread
 c. discuss
 d. tax

17. *Auspices* comes closest to meaning:
 a. authority
 b. logo
 c. deadline
 d. criticism

18. *Recalcitrant* comes closest to meaning:
   a. repetitive
   b. questioning
   c. obstinate
   d. impressive

19. *Irony* comes closest to meaning:
   a. truth of the matter
   b. original story
   c. dangerous fact
   d. incongruous, unexpected development

20. *Prodigy* comes closest to meaning:
   a. remarkably talented young child
   b. attentive student
   c. professional performer
   d. computer expert

21. *Plebeian* comes closest to meaning:
   a. complicated
   b. common
   c. idealistic
   d. unrealistic

22. *Proponent* comes closest to meaning:
   a. alterer
   b. prophet
   c. supporter
   d. detractor

23. *Austere* comes closest to meaning:
   a. luxurious and extravagant
   b. simple and stripped down to essentials
   c. attentive and detail-oriented
   d. relaxed and effective

24. *Priority* comes closest to meaning:
   a. arrange in order of relative importance
   b. carefully review
   c. thoroughly circulate
   d. discuss with others

25. *Prognosticator* comes closest to meaning:
   a. expert
   b. prophet
   c. politician
   d. writer

26. *Equanimity* comes closest to meaning:
   a. confidence
   b. poise
   c. irritation
   d. anger

27. *Amorphous* comes closest to meaning:
   a. exciting
   b. shapeless
   c. primitive
   d. overbearing

28. *Autonomy* comes closest to meaning:
   a. instruction
   b. independence
   c. supervision
   d. order

29. *Prototype* comes closest to meaning:
   a. fantasy
   b. deviation from established procedure
   c. early working model
   d. fragment of a previous model

30. *Lucid* comes closest to meaning:
   a. clear
   b. antagonistic
   c. long-winded
   d. hard to hear

31. *Collusion* comes closest to meaning:
   a. illicit action and deception among two or more people
   b. theft of another's inventory
   c. neglect of duty
   d. bribery of public officials

32. *Avarice* comes closest to meaning:
- **a.** high standards
- **b.** dreariness
- **c.** lack of attention to detail
- **d.** greed

33. *Melancholy* comes closest to meaning:
- **a.** ruthless
- **b.** sad
- **c.** dishonest
- **d.** disloyal

34. *Conjecture* comes closest to meaning:
- **a.** genius
- **b.** nonsense
- **c.** desperation
- **d.** guesswork

35. *Sophistry* comes closest to meaning:
- **a.** deceptive or misleading reasoning
- **b.** antagonistic exchanges
- **c.** fantastic exaggeration
- **d.** persistent disorganization

36. *Biennially* comes closest to meaning:
- **a.** twice a year
- **b.** twice a month
- **c.** every two months
- **d.** every two years

37. *Volatile* comes closest to meaning:
- **a.** transitory and unpredictable
- **b.** forgiving and understanding
- **c.** dishonest and deceitful
- **d.** incoherent and hard to understand

38. *Sanguine* comes closest to meaning:
- **a.** unrealistic
- **b.** hopeful
- **c.** disappointed
- **d.** devious

39. *Crestfallen* comes closest to meaning:
- **a.** joyous
- **b.** surprised
- **c.** disappointed
- **d.** uneasy

40. *Emigrate* comes closest to meaning:
- **a.** arrive in a new country
- **b.** leave one's country
- **c.** arrange for an ocean passage
- **d.** make a long journey to a foreign land

41. *Auspicious* comes closest to meaning:
- **a.** dangerous
- **b.** predictable
- **c.** happy
- **d.** logical

42. *Broach* comes closest to meaning:
- **a.** bring up
- **b.** review
- **c.** examine
- **d.** exhaust

43. *Obfuscation* comes closest to meaning:
- **a.** an attempt to reorganize a plan according to one's own wishes
- **b.** an attempt to confuse or mislead others
- **c.** an attempt to take credit for something that is not yours
- **d.** an attempt to enrage someone for no good reason

44. *Dilatory* comes closest to meaning:
- **a.** procrastinating
- **b.** irresponsible
- **c.** inattentive
- **d.** wordy

45. *Compunction* comes closest to meaning:
- **a.** reservation
- **b.** authority
- **c.** enthusiasm
- **d.** inspiration

46. *Fait accompli* comes closest to meaning:
  a. something that overlooks important quality concerns
  b. something that lulls people into a false sense of security
  c. something that has been shown to be an utter failure
  d. something that has already been completed and cannot be reversed

47. *Acute* comes closest to meaning:
  a. expected
  b. intense
  c. minor
  d. unpredicted

48. *Unprecedented* comes closest to meaning:
  a. unparalleled
  b. disappointing
  c. predictable
  d. profitable

49. *Élan* comes closest to meaning:
  a. punctuality and attentiveness
  b. enthusiasm and good spirit
  c. tact and discretion
  d. disappointment and bitterness

50. *Paradoxical* comes closest to meaning:
  a. mutually illuminating
  b. contradictory
  c. well reasoned
  d. old-fashioned

51. *Polygon* comes closest to meaning:
  a. superior example
  b. geometric figure
  c. military headquarters
  d. perfect square

52. *Ennui* comes closest to meaning:
  a. boredom
  b. resolve
  c. intelligence
  d. inspiration

53. *Salient* comes closest to meaning:
  a. perfect
  b. stranded
  c. important
  d. attentive to details

54. *Obsequious* comes closest to meaning:
  a. empty
  b. unintelligent
  c. fawning
  d. inflexible

55. *Indivious* comes closest to meaning:
  a. showing envy
  b. incorrect
  c. satanic
  d. enslaved

56. *Elixir* comes closest to meaning:
  a. crossroads

61. *Sycophant* comes closest to meaning:
  a. flatterer
  b. wealthy individual
  c. trusted elder
  d. unseen conspirator

62. *Irascible* most nearly means:
  a. flirtatious
  b. quiet
  c. irritable
  d. underhanded

63. *Sacrosanct* most nearly means:
  a. strange and wonderful
  b. sacred and venerated
  c. hedonistic and indulgent
  d. ancient and long-forgotten

64. *Epochal* most nearly means:
  a. momentous
  b. featuring many characters

c. related to the Bible
d. underestimated

65. *Hubris* most nearly means:
a. pride
b. a small bone in the inner ear
c. doorway
d. lucrative activity

PROOFREADING SKILLS TEST

The following test will gauge your ability to catch typographical and spelling errors in text. This is, of course, an essential skill for the executive assistant, a person who is not infrequently the last person to sign off on a document before it heads out the door.

How many of the errors in the long passage below can you spot? A corrected version, with appropriate letters and punctuation highlighted with ***bold italics,*** appears at the end of this chapter. If you miss more than five of the highlighted items, you need to improve your proofreading skills.

Example:

Thereis a considerable, variation in phraseology among the various verisons of this famous address. See Barton Webb' essay "Lincoln At Gettysburg", which appears at the end of this volume, for more information on the textual issues invloved here.

Corrected version:

There is a considerable variation in phraseology among the various ver***si***ons of this famous address. See Barton Webb***'s*** essay "Lincoln ***a***t Gettysburg***,"*** which appears at the end of this volume, for more information on the textual issues inv***ol***ved here.

The following test deals with overt *spelling and punctuation errors only.* It does not ask you to provide acceptable alternate approaches in either of these areas for text that is already correct. In other words, if a part of the text could legitimately be rendered in another way (where *cannot* appears for the older formulation *can not,* for instance), you won't receive any credit for altering it.

The gettysburg Address
Four score and seven years ago our fathers brought forth on this continent a new nation, concieved in liberty, and dedicated to the preposition that all men are created equal..

Now we are engaged in a great civil war testing whether that nation, or any nation so concieved and so dedicated, can long endure. Were are met on a great battlefield of that war. We have comto dedicate a prtion of that field, as a final resting place for those whohere gave their lives that that that nation might live. It is altogether fittting and proper that we should do this.

But, in a larger sense, we cannot dedicate, we cannot conseccrate, we cannot hallow this ground. The brave men (lving and dead) who struggled here have consecrated it far above our poor power to add or detract. the world will little note nor long remember what we say here, but it can never forget what they did here. It is for us the livng, rahter, too be dedicated here to the unfinished work which they who fought here have thus far so nobly advanced It is rather for us to be here dedicate to that great task remaning before us: that from these honored dead we take increased devotion to that cause for which they gave the last full measure of devotion; that we here highly resolve that these dead shall not have died in vain; that this nation, under God, shall have a new birht of freedom, and that govrenment of the people, by the people, for the people, shall not perish from the earth

ENGLISH GRAMMAR AND USAGE TEST

Correct grammar is a must for anyone who hopes to represent an important executive. If you correctly answer fewer than 42 of the following questions, you should undertake a thorough review of your grammatical skills.

Example: Maureen and the rest of the_____requested a meeting with Mr. Smith.

The word that best fills the blank is:

a. employees'
b. employees
c. employee's
(The correct answer is *b.*)

1. Either Mel or Mark_____a copy of the minutes of the meeting.

   The word that best fills the blank is:

   a. have
   b. has
   c. possess

2. You are the kind of person_____whom I can rely.

   The word that best fills the blank is:

   a. on
   b. in
   c. to

3. Paul_____to think he would never hear from his brother again.

   The word that best fills the blank is:

   a. begun
   b. began
   c. like

4. We must all try_____improve our skills in this area.

   The word that best fills the blank is:

   a. and
   b. to
   c. too

5. Just between you and_____, there's not much doubt about the outcome of the meeting.

   The word that best fills the blank is:

   a. I
   b. me
   c. myself

6. Melanie reads very rapidly,_____a trained speed reader should.

   The word that best fills the blank is:

   a. as
   b. like
   c. what

7. I need you to return the contract as_____as you can.

   The word that best fills the blank is:

   a. quick
   b. quickly
   c. rapid

8. I'm tired; I think I'm going to have to go_____down.

   The word that best fills the blank is:

   a. lay
   b. lie
   c. lye

9. Neither Jim nor Maureen_____comfortable with the arrangement.

   The word that best fills the blank is:

   a. is
   b. are
   c. feel

10. The speaker maintained that there were_____government regulations in this area than in years past.

    The word that best fills the blank is:

    a. less
    b. fewer
    c. lesser

11. _____do you suppose is responsible for this?

    The word that best fills the blank is:

    a. Who
    b. Whom
    c. Whomever

12. _____do you think he would have called?

    The word that best fills the blank is:

    a. Who

b. Whom
c. Him

13. It all comes down to_____testimony you find most credible.

The word that best fills the blank is:

a. who's
b. whos
c. whose

14. _____not at all unusual to feel a little apprehensive during your first few days on the job.

The word that best fills the blank is:

a. Its
b. It's
c. Its'

15. Mel and Doreen were on hand to meet Fred and_____at the airport.

The word that best fills the blank is:

a. I
b. me
c. mine

16. America, he argued, has yet to undergo_____greatest challenge.

The word that best fills the blank is:

a. its
b. its'
c. it's

17. Bill was saddened_____the decision.

The word that best fills the blank is:

a. by
b. with
c. to

18. Eleanor is planning to take two_____paid vacation.

The word that best fills the blank is:

a. month's
b. months'
c. months

19. Bert was_____to ask for a raise when Mr. Smith offered him one.

The option that best fills the blank is:

a. already
b. all ready
c. allready

20. Michelle thinks she left something here—is that jacket_____?

The word that best fills the blank is:

a. her's
b. hers
c. hers'

21. The meeting emphasized that safety is_____responsibility.

The word that best fills the blank is:

a. everyone's
b. everyones
c. everybody

22. Recently I read in *Time* magazine_____gasoline prices are likely to be more volatile this year.

The word that best fills the blank is:

a. how
b. where
c. that

23. The proposal's greatest flaw_____its many inconsistencies.

The word that best fills the blank is:

a. are
b. is
c. were

24. One of my reasons for leaving the job last year_____the many hours I had to spend on the road.

The word that best fills the blank is:

a. was
b. were
c. is

25. His passion_____gourmet wines.

The word that best fills the blank is:

a. was
b. were
c. are

26. I learned this morning that neither the blue team nor the green team_____eligible for this year's playoffs.

The word that best fills the blank is:

a. is
b. were
c. got

27. _____go to the movies together.

The word that best fills the blank is:

a. Lets'
b. Let's
c. Lets

28. If you had_____for another mile, you would have seen the house.

The word that best fills the blank is:

a. drove
b. drived
c. driven

29. The marketing people wanted to know how many of_____suggestions were implemented.

The word that best fills the blank is:

a. their
b. there
c. they're

30. Diane wanted to know whether_____planning to go to summer camp this year.

The word that best fills the blank is:

a. your
b. you're
c. you

31. Jim, Paul, and Stan decided to wear_____most colorful ties.

The word that best fills the blank is:

a. their
b. they're
c. there

32. All_____closest friends are going to be attending the seminar.

The word that best fills the blank is:

a. you're
b. your
c. you

33. My friend Frank_____to vacation in Nantucket every year.

The word that best fills the blank is:

a. use
b. used
c. like

34. The overseers will be two homeowners, Mr. Smith and_____.

The word that best fills the blank is:

a. I
b. me
c. myself

35. Martin did a magnificent job of rowing, but Pat did just as_____.

The word that best fills the blank is:

a. good
b. well
c. fast

36. You can give that job to Ira; he_____care what lands on his desk.

The word that best fills the blank is:

a. don't
b. ain't
c. doesn't

37. The report lists up-to-date figures, but_____the graphics that we asked for.

The option that best fills the blank is:

a. where are
b. he left out
c. omits

38. My daughter's teacher insists that she_____her assignment before beginning Chapter 6.

The word that best fills the blank is:

a. rewrites
b. redoes
c. rewrite

39. _____still a good many issues to resolve.

The option that best fills the blank is:

a. There's
b. There are
c. There was

40. If only Jim_____here, he'd help us come up with the solution.

The word that best fills the blank is:

a. were
b. was
c. is

41. Mark says we_____be able to take the class now.

The word that best fills the blank is:

a. may
b. might
c. maybe

42. Walking in the door…

The option that best completes the sentence is:

a. …the wastebasket blocked my way.
b. …I found my way blocked by the wastebasket.
c. …someone had left the wastebasket right where I was walking.

43. Having secured his freedom at long last…

The option that best completes the sentence is:

a. …the prisoner's joy knew no bounds.
b. …joy was evident on the prisoner's face.
c. …the prisoner rejoiced.

44. Working 14 hours a day the way you do,…

The option that best completes the sentence is:

a. …I think you ought to follow my example and set up a less demanding schedule.
b. …you ought to follow my example and set up a less demanding schedule.
c. …your schedule ought to be less demanding.

45. The two sisters bore such a striking resemblance to each other that I…

The option that best completes the sentence is:

a. couldn't hardly tell them apart.
b. could hardly tell them apart.
c. hardly couldn't tell them apart.

46. Jeanne is the kind of person…

The option that best completes the sentence is:

a. …whom you can trust.
b. …that you can trust.
c. …who you can trust.

47. A formal contract…

The option that best completes the sentence is:

a. …is when two parties develop a written agreement.
b. …is a written agreement developed by two parties.
c. …is where two parties develop a written agreement.

48. The disturbing news reports could be the result of…

The option that best completes the sentence is:

a. …any number of phenomena.
b. …any phenomena that appears on the following list.
c. …any of the phenomenon we discussed yesterday.

49. Although the annual report showed that we posted a loss during our most recent fiscal year,...

The option that best completes the sentence is:
a. ...hopefully next year will be better.
b. ...we are hopeful that next year will be better.
c. ...next year will hopefully be better.

SPELLING SKILLS TEST

Two stark facts about the executive assistant's life are worth noting here. First, if you're not a great speller, you'd better become one fairly quickly. Second, *becoming* a great speller is not as difficult as many people seem to think. All it requires is the development of a healthy uncertainty about whether something has been set down correctly, and an attendant willingness to *stop and look the word up before passing the document along.* When combined with the knack for storing the properly spelled word in your memory so that the next time you come across it, you won't have to think twice about whether it "looks right," this skill is all that's necessary. I find that stopping and looking the word up is the step "genetic bad spellers" never seem to make the time for.

Here is a spelling test of 110 words. If you get more than 12 wrong, you probably need to work on your spelling skills...and perhaps strengthen your looking-it-up-in-the-first-place muscle.

1. a) abreviate b) abbreviate c) abreveiate d) abbreveate
2. a) peculiar b) pecullliar c) pekuliar d) paculiar
3. a) vississitiude b) vicisitude c) visisitude d) vicissitude
4. a) absence b) absens c) absense d) abscence
5. a) mayonnaise b) manaise c) mayonaise d) mayonaize
6. a) committment b) comitment c) commitment d) comittment
7. a) acordance b) accordance c) accordanse d) accordantce
8. a) specyfy b) spesify c) spessify d) specify

9. a) addmissable b) admissible c) admissable d) amisable
10. a) libiddinal b) libidinal c) libidianal d) libidinnal
11. a) vijilance b) vigilance c) vidgilance d) vigelance
12. a) tarriff b) tarif c) tarrif d) tariff
13. a) phisycian b) physician c) fisician d) physition
14. a) aile b) ile c) aisle d) aiasle
15. a) doshund b) dachshund c) daushund d) dachshond
16. a) larceny b) larseny c) larcenie d) larsonie
17. a) liquafaction b) liquifaction c) liquefaction d) liquefacshen
18. a) pakyderm b) pachyderm c) pachydurm d) pacquederm
19. a) alotted b) allotted c) alloted d) aloted
20. a) medieval b) mideaval c) medievil d) midiaeval
21. a) allowants b) allowance c) allowanse d) alowance
22. a) miniscule b) minuscule c) minuschule d) minuscul
23. a) amateurish b) amaturish c) amaterish d) amatureish
24. a) padestrian b) pedestrain c) pedestrian d) pidestrian
25. a) renumerration b) remuneration c) remuneraytion d) renumeraschion
26. a) miniaturization b) minituriazation c) minuturization d) miniaturazation
27. a) auxiliary b) oxiliary c) augsiliary d) auxcilliary
28. a) catastrofe b) catastrophy c) catastrophe d) cattastrophee
29. a) leppord b) leopard c) lepperd d) leoperd
30. a) changeable b) changable c) changible d) changibel
31. a) leegion b) legion c) lejion d) leigion
32. a) carberetor b) carburator c) carbueretor d) carburetor
33. a) dispite b) despyte c) dispyte d) despite
34. a) certifiable b) certifyable c) certifable d) certifyible
35. a) clientele b) clientell c) clyentele d) clientel
36. a) beneficial b) benefisial c) benefishial d) benificial

37. a) stelth b) stealth c) steallth d) steolth
38. a) pinance b) pennance c) penince d) penance
39. a) contemptable b) contemptible c) contemtable d) contemputble
40. a) dispair b) despare c) despaire d) despair
41. a) milage b) milege c) mileage d) myleage
42. a) embaras b) embarrass c) embarras d) embarass
43. a) dirision b) derision c) deresion d)deirision
44. a) unconstitutional b) unconstitutionall c) unconstetutional d) unconstittutional
45. a) enchilada b) enchelada c) enchylada d) enchehlada
46. a) sincopate b) syncopayte c) syncopate d) sincopait
47. a) legacy b) leggacy c) legasy d) legassy
48. a) idiocynracy b) idiosynkrasy c) idiosyncrasy d) ideosyncrasy
49. a) penurious b) pennurious c) penyurious d) penerious
50. a) greivous b) grevous c) grievious d) grievous
51. a) popurree b) potpourri c) potporri d) popourri
52. a) technicality b) techniciality c) techniquality d) techinicality
53. a) stacato b) stacatto c) staccato d) staccatto
54. a) decadence b) decadens c) decadants d) deckadance
55. a) economacal b) econamical c) economicial d) economical
56. a) irridescent b) iridescent c) irridesent d) iridesent
57. a) celophane b) cellophane c) cellofane d) cellophain
58. a) dossiay b) dossie c) dossier d) dosier
59. a) ganggrene b) gangrene c) gangreene d) gangreen
60. a) pageantry b) padgeantry c) pageontry d) pagiantry
61. a) questionaire b) questioneire c) questionnaire d) questionneire
62. a) intravenous b) intrevenous c) intravenus d) intravenious

63. a) phanatacism b) fanaticism c) fanatacism d) fantacism

64. a) sperical b) spherical c) spherickal d) spheracle

65. a) counterinteligence b) countrintelligence c) counter-intelligence d) counterintelligience

66 a) posthumous b) posthumus c) posthumuous d) postu-mous

67. a) percieve b) persieve c) perseive d) perceive

68. a) catalist b) catalyst c) catelyst d) katalyst

69. a) sucotash b) succotash c) sucottash d) succottash

70. a) interdikt b) intercdict c) interdict d) intredicte

71. a) wierd b) weird c) weerd d) weard

72. a) purpoise b) porpose c)porpuss d) porpoise

73. a) cieling b) ceiling c) ceeling d) celing

74. a) suffrage b) sufferage c) suffereage d) suffereadge

75. a) nieghbor b) neighbur c) neighbor d) neighbore

76. a) eucaliptus b) eucalliptus c) eucalyptus d) eucaliptius

77. a) dishevelled b) dissheveled c) disshevelled d) disheveled

78. a) quizical b) quizzical c) quizzicle d) quizicle

79. a) intoxickant b) intoxacant c) intoxicant d) intoxicante

80. a) wiegh b) weigh c) waigh d) weygh

81. a) coyote b) coyotte c) ciyote d) koyote

82. a) exhileration b) exhilharation c) exhilaration d) exilha-ration

83. a) persuasive b) perswaysive c) persuacive d) persuaysive

84. a) gadflie b) gadfly c) gaddfly d) gadfli

85. a) intermedary b) intermediary c) intermediarie d) inter-midiary

86. a) irascible b) irasible c) irascibel d) irascable

87. a) unanimiously b) unanimously c) unanamously d) unan-imissly

88. a) tobbacco b) tobacco c) tobaco d) tobbaco

89. a) caffeine b) cafeine c) caffiene d) cafiene

90. a) benificent b) beneficent c) beneficient d) benefiecient

91. a) suficient b) sufficeint c) sufficient d) sufficiant
92. a) poridge b) porridge c) porridj d) porige
93. a) irksome b) erksome c) urksome d) earksome
94. a) holyness b) holliness c) holiness b) holeyness
95. a) benafactor b) benefactor c) bennefactor d) benifactor
96. a) suttle b) sutle c) sutile c) subtle
97. a) efervescent b) effervessent c) effervecent d) effervescent
98. a) predeliction b) predilection c) predelicition d) predelection
99. a) invision b) innvision c) envission d) envision
100. a) consensus b) concensus c) consensuss d) consentsus
101. a) tryumvirate b) triumvarate c) triumvirate
102. a) height b) heighth c) hieght
103. a) iconoclastic b) iconoclasstic c) iconoclastick
104. a) supersede b) supercede c) superceed
105. a) obfescation b) obfuscation c) obfuscaytion
106. a) eufemism b) uphemism c) euphemism
107. a) sicophant b) sycophand c) sycophant
108. a) antiphon b) antiphone c) antifon
109. a) resillient b) resiliant c) resilient
110. a) appurtenance b) appertenince c) appertinents

ANSWERS

VOCABULARY SKILLS TEST

1. Omnipotent comes closest to meaning:
   <u>**a.** all-powerful</u>
   b. frustrated
   c. relaxed
   d. attentive

2. *Altruism* comes closest to meaning:
   a. sarcasm
   b. intelligence
   c. generosity
   d. open-mindedness
3. *Stringent* comes closest to meaning:
   a. elaborate
   b. unimaginative
   c. professional
   d. strict
4. *Bemused* comes closest to meaning:
   a. preoccupied
   b. disturbed
   c. confused
   d. uninterested
5. *Infer* comes closest to meaning:
   a. conclude
   b. imply
   c. decide
   d. begin
6. Capriciously comes closest to meaning:
   a. joyously
   b. impulsively
   c. predictably
   d. hilariously
7. Reciprocate comes closest to meaning:
   a. seek vengeance
   b. act hastily
   c. respond in kind
   d. act as mediator
8. Intercede comes closest to meaning:
   a. volunteer
   b. step in
   c. interrogate
   d. undermine

9. *Abrogated* comes closest to meaning:
   a. invalidated
   b. completed
   c. reread
   d. overseen

10. *Specious* comes closest to meaning:
    a. intelligent
    b. misleading
    c. loud
    d. bitter

11. *Stereotypes* comes closest to meaning:
    a. double meanings
    b. predictable descriptions
    c. powerful images
    d. plot twists

12. *Surreptitious* comes closest to meaning:
    a. intolerant
    b. rude
    c. secret
    d. disruptive

13. *Retrospect* comes closest to meaning:
    a. truth
    b. hindsight
    c. fairness
    d. summary

14. *Strident* comes closest to meaning:
    a. detailed
    b. harsh
    c. brief
    d. sentimental

15. *Tenuous* comes closest to meaning:
    a. attentive
    b. logical
    c. weak
    d. dangerous

16. *Excise* comes closest to meaning:
   a. eliminate
   b. proofread
   c. discuss
   d. tax

17. *Auspices* comes closest to meaning:
   a. authority
   b. logo
   c. deadline
   d. criticism

18. *Recalcitrant* comes closest to meaning:
   a. repetitive
   b. questioning
   c. obstinate
   d. impressive

19. *Irony* comes closest to meaning:
   a. truth of the matter
   b. original story
   c. dangerous fact
   d. incongruous, unexpected development

20. *Prodigy* comes closest to meaning:
   a. remarkably talented young child
   b. attentive student
   c. professional performer
   d. computer expert

21. *Plebeian* comes closest to meaning:
   a. complicated
   b. common
   c. idealistic
   d. unrealistic

22. *Proponent* comes closest to meaning:
   a. alterer
   b. prophet
   c. supporter
   d. detractor

23. *Austere* comes closest to meaning:
   a. luxurious and extravagant
   b. simple and stripped down to essentials
   c. attentive and detail-oriented
   d. relaxed and effective

24. *Prioritize* comes closest to meaning:
   a. arrange in order of importance
   b. carefully review
   c. thoroughly circulate
   d. discuss with others

25. *Prognosticator* comes closest to meaning:
   a. expert
   b. prophet
   c. politician
   d. writer

26. *Equanimity* comes closest to meaning:
   a. confidence
   b. poise
   c. irritation
   d. anger

27. *Amorphous* comes closest to meaning:
   a. exciting
   b. shapeless
   c. primitive
   d. overbearing

28. *Autonomy* comes closest to meaning:
   a. instruction
   b. independence
   c. supervision
   d. order

29. *Prototype* comes closest to meaning:
   a. fantasy
   b. deviation from established procedure
   c. early working model
   d. fragment of a previous model

30. *Lucid* comes closest to meaning:

a. clear
b. antagonistic
c. long-winded
d. hard to hear

31. *Collusion* comes closest to meaning:

a. illicit action and deception among two or more people
b. theft of another's inventory
c. neglect of duty
d. bribery of public officials

32. *Avarice* comes closest to meaning:

a. high standards
b. dreariness
c. lack of attention to detail
d. greed

33. *Melancholy* comes closest to meaning:

a. ruthless
b. sad
c. dishonest
d. disloyal

34. *Conjecture* comes closest to meaning:

a. genius
b. nonsense
c. desperation
d. guesswork

35. *Sophistry* comes closest to meaning:

a. deceptive or misleading reasoning
b. antagonistic exchanges
c. fantastic exaggeration
d. persistent disorganization

36. *Biennially* comes closest to meaning:

a. twice a year
b. twice a month
c. every two months
d. every two years

37. *Volatile* comes closest to meaning:
   a. transitory and unpredictable
   b. forgiving and understanding
   c. dishonest and deceitful
   d. incoherent and hard to understand

38. *Sanguine* comes closest to meaning:
   a. unrealistic
   b. hopeful
   c. disappointed
   d. devious

39. *Crestfallen* comes closest to meaning:
   a. joyous
   b. surprised
   c. disappointed
   d. uneasy

40. *Emigrate* comes closest to meaning:
   a. arrive in a new country
   b. leave one's country
   c. arrange for an ocean passage
   d. make a long journey to a foreign land

41. *Auspicious* comes closest to meaning:
   a. dangerous
   b. predictable
   c. happy
   d. logical

42. *Broach* comes closest to meaning:
   a. bring up
   b. review
   c. examine
   d. exhaust

43. *Obfuscation* comes closest to meaning:
   a. an attempt to reorganize a plan according to one's own wishes
   b. an attempt to confuse or mislead others
   c. an attempt to take credit for something that is not yours
   d. an attempt to enrage someone for no good reason

44. *Dilatory* comes closest to meaning:

a. procrastinating
b. irresponsible
c. inattentive
d. wordy

45. *Compunction* comes closest to meaning:

a. reservation
b. authority
c. enthusiasm
d. inspiration

46. *Fait accompli* comes closest to meaning:

a. something that overlooks important quality concerns
b. something that lulls people into a false sense of security
c. something that has been shown to be an utter failure
d. something that has already been completed and cannot be reversed

47. *Acute* comes closest to meaning:

a. expected
b. intense
c. minor
d. unpredicted

48. *Unprecedented* comes closest to meaning:

a. unparalleled
b. disappointing
c. predictable
d. profitable

49. *Élan* comes closest to meaning:

a. punctuality and attentivness
b. enthusiasm and good spirit
c. tact and discretion
d. disappointment and bitterness

50. *Paradoxical* comes closest to meaning:

a. mutually illuminating
b. contradictory
c. well reasoned
d. old-fashioned

51. *Polygon* comes closest to meaning:
   a. superior example
   b. geometric figure
   c. military headquarters
   d. perfect square

52. *Ennui* comes closest to meaning:
   a. boredom
   b. resolve
   c. intelligence
   d. inspiration

53. *Salient* comes closest to meaning:
   a. perfect
   b. stranded
   c. important
   d. attentive to details

54. *Obsequious* comes closest to meaning:
   a. empty
   b. unintelligent
   c. fawning
   d. inflexible

55. *Invidious* comes closest to meaning:
   a. showing envy
   b. incorrect
   c. satanic
   d. enslaved

56. *Elixir* comes closest to meaning:
   a. crossroads
   b. potion
   c. farewell
   d. youthful vigor

57. *Nebulous* comes closest to meaning:
   a. indistinct
   b. specific
   c. vacant
   d. untrustworthy

58. *Maelstrom* comes closest to meaning:
   a. conflict
   b. interruption
   c. whirlpool
   d. injury

59. *Malaise* comes closest to meaning:
   a. epidemic
   b. depression
   c. innovation
   d. revision

60. *Causalty* comes closest to meaning:
   a. death or injury in battle
   b. freshness
   c. interrelation between cause and effect
   d. forgiveness

61. *Sycophant* comes closest to meaning:
   a. flatterer
   b. wealthy individual
   c. trusted elder
   d. unseen conspirator

62. *Irascible* most nearly means:
   a. flirtatious
   b. quiet
   c. irritable
   d. underhanded

63. *Sacrosanct* most nearly means:
   a. strange and wonderful
   b. sacred and venerated
   c. hedonistic and indulgent
   d. ancient and long-forgotten

64. *Epochal* most nearly means:
   a. momentous
   b. featuring many characters
   c. related to the Bible
   d. underestimated

65. *Hubris* most nearly means:
   a. pride
   b. small bone in the inner ear
   c. doorway
   d. lucrative activity

PROOFREADING SKILLS TEST

The **G**ettysburg Address

Four score and seven years ago our fathers brought forth on this continent a new nation, conc***ei***ved in liberty, and dedicated to the pr***o***position that all men are created equal.

No***w*** ***w***e are engaged in a great civil war, testing whether that nation, or any nation so conc***ei***ved and so dedicated, can long endure. We ***[note deletion of*** *re*] are met on a great battlefield of that war. We have co***me*** ***t***o dedicate a p***o***rtion of that field, as a final resting place for those wh***o*** ***h***ere gave their lives that that ***[note deletion of third*** **that**] nation might live. It is altogether fitting ***[note deletion of extra*** *t*] and proper that we should do this.

But, in a larger sense, we cannot dedicate, we cannot consecrate, ***[note deletion of extra*** *c*] we cannot hallow this ground. The brave men (l***i***ving and dead) who struggled here have consecrated it far above our poor power to add or detract. ***T***he world will little note nor long remember what we say here, but it can never forget what they did here. It is for us the li***v***ing, ra***th***er, ***to*** be dedicated here to the unfinished work which they who fought here have thus far so nobly advanced. It is rather for us to be here dedicate***d*** to that great task rema***i***ning before us: that from these honored dead we take increased devotion to that cause for which they gave the last full measure of devotion; that we here highly resolve that these dead shall not have died in vain; that this nation, under God, shall have a new bir***th*** of freedom, and that gov***ern***ment of the people, by the people, for the people, shall not perish from the earth.

ENGLISH GRAMMAR AND USAGE TEST

1. Either Mel or Mark_____a copy of the minutes of the meeting.

   The word that best fills the blank is:

   a. have

   b. has

   c. possess

2. You are the kind of person_____whom I can rely.

   The word that best fills the blank is:

   a. on

   b. in

   c. to

3. Paul_____to think he would never hear from his brother again.

   The word that best fills the blank is:

   a. begun

   b. began

   c. like

4. We must all try_____improve our skills in this area.

   The word that best fills the blank is:

   a. and

   b. to

   c. too

5. Just between you and_____, there's not much doubt about the outcome of the meeting.

   The word that best fills the blank is:

   a. I

   b. me

   c. myself

6. Melanie reads very rapidly,_____a trained speed reader should.

   The word that best fills the blank is:

   a. as

   b. like

   c. what

7. I need you to return the contract as_____as you can.

   The word that best fills the blank is:

   a. quick
   <u>b. quickly</u>
   c. rapid

8. I'm tired; I think I'm going to have to go_____down.

   The word that best fills the blank is:

   a. lay
   <u>b. lie</u>
   c. lye

9. Neither Jim nor Maureen_____comfortable with the arrangement.

   The word that best fills the blank is:

   <u>a. is</u>
   b. are
   c. feel

10. The speaker maintained that there were_____government regulations in this area than in years past.

    The word that best fills the blank is:

    a. less
    <u>b. fewer</u>
    c. lesser

11. _____do you suppose is responsible for this?

    The word that best fills the blank is:

    <u>a. Who</u>
    b. Whom
    c. Whomever

12. _____do you think he would have called?

    The word that best fills the blank is:

    a. Who
    <u>b. Whom</u>
    c. Him

13. It all comes down to_____testimony you find most credible.

    The word that best fills the blank is:

    a. who's

b. whos
c. whose

14. _____not at all unusual to feel a little apprehensive during your first few days on the job.

The word that best fills the blank is:
a. Its
b. It's
c. Its'

15. Mel and Doreen were on hand to meet Fred and_____at the airport.

The word that best fills the blank is:
a. I
b. me
c. mine

16. America, he argued, has yet to undergo_____greatest challenge.

The word that best fills the blank is:
a. its
b. its'
c. it's

17. Bill was saddened_____the decision.

The word that best fills the blank is:
a. by
b. with
c. to

18. Eleanor is planning to take two_____paid vacation.

The word that best fills the blank is:
a. month's
b. months'
c. months

19. Bert was_____to ask for a raise when Mr. Smith offered him one.

The option that best fills the blank is:
a. already
b. all ready
c. allready

20. Michelle thinks she left something here—is that jacket_____?

The word that best fills the blank is:

a. her's

b. hers

c. hers'

21. The meeting emphasized that safety is_____responsibility.

The word that best fills the blank is:

a. everyone's

b. everyones

c. everybody

22. Recently I read in *Time* magazine_____gasoline prices are likely to be more volatile this year.

The word that best fills the blank is:

a. how

b. where

c. that

23. The proposal's greatest flaw_____its many inconsistencies.

The word that best fills the blank is:

a. are

b. is

c. were

24. One of my reasons for leaving the job last year_____the many hours I had to spend on the road.

The word that best fills the blank is:

a. was

b. were

c. is

25. His passion_____gourmet wines.

The word that best fills the blank is:

a. was

b. were

c. are

26. I learned this morning that neither the blue team nor the green team_____eligible for this year's playoffs.

The word that best fills the blank is:
a. is
b. were
c. got

27. _____go to the movies together.

The word that best fills the blank is:
a. Lets'
b. Let's
c. Lets

28. If you had_____for another mile, you would have seen the house.

The word that best fills the blank is:
a. drove
b. drived
c. driven

29. The marketing people wanted to know how many of _____suggestions were implemented.

The word that best fills the blank is:
a. their
b. there
c. they're

30. Diane wanted to know whether_____ planning to go to summer camp this year.

The word that best fills the blank is:
a. your
b. you're
c. you

31. Jim, Paul, and Stan decided to wear_____most colorful ties.

The word that best fills the blank is:
a. their
b. they're
c. there

32. All_____closest friends are going to be attending the seminar.

The word that best fills the blank is:
a. you're
b. your
c. you

33. My friend Frank_____to vacation in Nantucket every year.

The word that best fills the blank is:
a. use
b. used
c. like

34. The overseers will be two homeowners, Mr. Smith and_____.

The word that best fills the blank is:
a. I
b. me
c. myself

35. Martin did a magnificent job of rowing, but Pat did just as_____.

The word that best fills the blank is:
a. good
b. well
c. fast

36. You can give that job to Ira; he_____care what lands on his desk.

The word that best fills the blank is:
a. don't
b. ain't
c. doesn't

37. The report lists up-to-date figures, but_____the graphics that we asked for.

The option that best fills the blank is:
a. where are
b. he left out
c. omits

38. My daughter's teacher insists that she_____her assignment before beginning Chapter 6.

The word that best fills the blank is:

a. rewrites
b. redoes
c. rewrite

39. _____still a good many issues to resolve.

The option that best fills the blank is:
a. There's
b. There are
c. There was

40. If only Jim_____here, he'd help us come up with the solution.

The word that best fills the blank is:
a. were
b. was
c. is

41. Mark says we_____be able to take the class now.

The word that best fills the blank is:
a. may
b. might
c. maybe

42. Walking in the door...

The option that best completes the sentence is:
a. ...the wastebasket blocked my way.
b. ...I found my way blocked by the wastebasket.
c. ...someone had left the wastebasket right where I was walking.

43. Having secured his freedom at long last...

The option that best completes the sentence is:
a. ...the prisoner's joy knew no bounds.
b. ...joy was evident on the prisoner's face.
c. ...the prisoner rejoiced.

44. Working 14 hours a day the way you do,...

The option that best completes the sentence is:
a. ...I think you ought to follow my example and set up a less demanding schedule.
b. ...you ought to follow my example and set up a less demanding schedule.

c. ...your schedule ought to be less demanding.

45. The two sisters bore such a striking resemblance to each other that I...

The option that best completes the sentence is:
a. couldn't hardly tell them apart.
b. could hardly tell them apart.
c. hardly couldn't tell them apart.

46. Jeanne is the kind of person...

The option that best completes the sentence is:
a. ...whom you can trust.
b. ...that you can trust.
c. ...who you can trust.

47. A formal contract...

The option that best completes the sentence is:
a. ...is when two parties develop a written agreement.
b. ...is a written agreement developed by two parties.
c. ...is where two parties develop a written agreement.

48. The disturbing news reports could be the result of...

The option that best completes the sentence is:
a. ...any number of phenomena.
b. ...any phenomena that appears on the following list.
c. ...any of the phenomenon we discussed yesterday.

49. Although the annual report showed that we posted a loss during our most recent fiscal year,...

The option that best completes the sentence is:
a. ...hopefully next year will be better.
b. ...we are hopeful that next year will be better.
c. ...next year will hopefully be better.

SPELLING SKILLS TEST

1. a) abreviate b) abbreviate c) abreveiate d) abbreveate
2. a) peculiar b) peculliar c) pekuliar d) paculiar
3. a) vississitiude b) vicisitude c) visisitude d) vicissitude
4. a) absence b) absens c) absense d) abscence

5. a) mayonnaise b) manaise c) mayonaise d) mayonaize
6. a) committment b) comitment c) commitment d) comittment
7. a) acordance b) accordance c) accordanse d) accordantce
8. a) specyfy b) spesify c) spessify d) specify
9. a) addmissable b) admissible c) admissable d) amisable
10. a) libiddinal b) libidinal c) libidianal d) libidinnal
11. a) vijilance b) vigilance c) vidgilance d) vigelance
12. a) tarriff b) tarif c) tarrif d) tariff
13. a) phisycian b) physician c) fisician d) physition
14. a) aile b) ile c) aisle d) aiasle
15. a) doshund b) dachshund c) daushund d) dachshond
16. a) larceny b) larseny c) larcenie d) larsonie
17. a) liquafaction b) liquifaction c) liquefaction d) liquefacshen
18. a) pakyderm b) pachyderm c) pachydurm d) pacquederm
19. a) alotted b) allotted c) alloted d) aloted
20. a) medieval b) mideaval c) medievil d) midiaeval
21. a) allowants b) allowance c) allowanse d) alowance
22. a) miniscule b) minuscules c) minuschule d) minuscul
23. a) amateurish b) amaturish c) amaterish d) amatureish
24. a) padestrian b) pedestrain c) pedestrian d) pidestrian
25. a) renumerration b) remuneration c) remuneraytion d) renumeraschion
26. a) miniaturization b) minituriazation c) minuturization d) miniaturazation
27. a) auxiliary b) oxiliary c) augsiliary d) auxcilliary
28. a) catastrofe b) catastrophy c) catastrophe d) cattastrophee
29. a) leppord b) leopard c) lepperd d) leoperd
30. a) changeable b) changable c) changible d) changibel
31. a) leegion b) legion c) lejion d) leigion

32. a) carberetor b) carburator c) carbueretor d) carburetor
33. a) dispite b) despyte c) dispyte d) despite
34. a) certifiable b) certifyable c) certifable d) certifyible
35. a) clientele b) clientell c) clyentele d) clientel
36. a) beneficial b) benefisial c) benefishial d) benificial
37. a) stelth b) stealth c) steallth d) steolth
38. a) pinance b) pennance c) penince d) penance
39. a) contemptable b) contemptible c) contemtable d) contemputble
40. a) dispair b) despare c) despaire d) despair
41. a) milage b) milege c) mileage d)myleage
42. a) embaras b) embarrass c) embarras d) embarass
43. a) dirision b) derision c) deresion d) deirision
44. a) unconstitutional b) unconstitutionall c) unconstetutional d) unconstittutional
45. a) enchilada b) enchelada c) enchylada d) enchehlada
46. a) sincopate b) syncopayte c) syncopate d) sincopait
47. a) legacy b) leggacy c) legasy d) legassy
48. a) idiocynracy b) idiosynkrasy c) idiosyncrasy d)ideosyncrasy
49. a) penurious b) pennurious c) penyurious d) penerious
50. a) greivous b) grevous c) grievious d) grievous
51. a) popurree b) potpourri c) potporri d) popourri
52. a) technicality b) techniciality c) techniquality d) techinicality
53. a) stacato b) stacatto c) staccato d) staccatto
54. a) decadence b) decadens c) decadants d) deckadance
55. a) economacal b) econamical c) economicial d) economical
56. a) irridescent b) iridescent c) irridesent d) iridesent
57. a) celophane b) cellophane c) cellofane d) cellophain
58. a) dossiay b) dossie c) dossier d) dosier

59. a) ganggrene b) gangrene c) gangreene d) gangreen

60. a) pageantry b) padgeantry c) pageontry d) pagiantry

61. a) questionaire b) questioneire c) questionnaire d) questionneire

62. a) intravenous b) intrevenous c) intravenus d) intravenious

63. a) phanatacism b) fanaticism c) fanatacism d) fantacism

64. a) sperical b) spherical c) spherickal d) spheracle

65. a) counterinteligence b) countrintelligence c) counterintelligence d) counterintelligience

66. a) posthumous b) posthumus c) posthumuous d) postumous

67. a) percieve b) persieve c) perseive d) perceive

68. a) catalist b) catalyst c) catelyst d) katalyst

69. a) sucotash b) succotash c) sucottash d) succottash

70. a) interdikt b) interedict c) interdict d) intredicte

71. a) wierd b) weird c) weerd d) weard

72. a) purpoise b) porpose c) porpuss d) porpoise

73. a) cieling b) ceiling c) ceeling d) celing

74. a) suffrage b) sufferage c) suffereage d) suffereadge

75. a) nieghbor b) neighbur c) neighbor d) neighbore

76. a) eucaliptus b) eucalliptus c) eucalyptus d) eucaliptius

77. a) dishevelled b) dissheveled c) disshevelled d) disheveled

78. a) quizical b) quizzical c) quizzicle d) quizicle

79. a) intoxickant b) intoxacant c) intoxicant d) intoxicante

80. a) wiegh b) weigh c) waigh d) weygh

81. a) coyote b) coyotte c) ciyote d) koyote

82. a) exhileration b) exhilharation c) exhilaration d) exilharation

83. a) persuasive b) perswaysive c) persuacive d) persuaysive

84. a) gadflie b) gadfly c) gaddfly d) gadfli

85. a) intermedary b) intermediary c) intermediarie d) intermidiary
86. a) irascible b) irasible c) irascibel d) irascable
87. a) unanimiously b) unanimously c) unanamously d) unanimissly
88. a) tobbacco b) tobacco c) tobaco d) tobbaco
89. a) caffeine b) cafeine c) caffiene d) cafiene
90. a) benificent b) beneficent c) beneficient d) benefiecient
91. a) suficient b) sufficeint c) sufficient d) sufficiant
92. a) poridge b) porridge c) porridj d) porige
93. a) irksome b) erksome c) urksome d) earksome
94. a) holyness b) holliness c) holiness b) holeyness
95. a) benafactor b) benefactor c) bennefactor d) benifactor
96. a) suttle b) sutle c) sutile d) subtle
97. a) efervescent b) effervessent c) effervecent d) effervescent
98. a) predeliction b) predilection c) predelicition d) predelection
99. a) invision b) innvision c) envission d) envision
100. a) consensus b) concensus c) consensuss d) consentsus
101. a) tryumvirate b) triumvarate c) triumvirate
102. a) height b) heighth c) hieght
103. a) iconoclastic b) iconoclasstic c) iconoclastick
104. a) supersede b) supercede c) superceed
105. a) obfescation b) obfuscation c) obfuscaytion
106. a) eufemism b) uphemism c) euphemism
107. a) sicophant b) sycophand c) sycophant
108. a) antiphon b) antiphone c) antifon
109. a) resillient b) resiliant c) resilient
110. a) appurtenance b) appertenince c) appertinents
111. a) iconoclast b) ikonoclast c) icanoclast
112. a) iggneous b) igneous c) igneus

113. a) imminent b) iminent c) iminant

114. a) paraphraze b) parafrase c) paraphrase

115. a) ziggurat b) zigurat c) zigarat

116. a) fulcrum b) fullcrum c) fulcrumb

117. a) impecuneous b) impecunious c) impecunious

118. a) imbroglio b) imbrollio c) imbrogglio

119. a) imperseptible b) imperceptible c) imperceptable

120. a) proffligacy b) profligacy c) proflagacy

121. a) wreaking b) wreeking c) wreaquing

122. a) efemeral b) epheremal c)ephemeral

INDEX